THE POWER OF TODA(Y)²

The Power *of* **TODA(*y*)²**
Get the most out of TODAY for better tomorrows

ISBN 979-11-964106-4-3 (03190)

Published by yemmibooks

Hasung Plaza #601, 1568, Jungang-ro, Ilsanseo-gu, Goyang-si, Gyeonggi-do,
Republic of Korea
yemmibooks@naver.com

Printed in Korea

A CIP catalogue record of the National Library of Korea for this book is available at
the homepage of CIP(http://seoji.nl.go.kr) and Korean Library Information System
Network(http://www.nl.go.kr/kolisnet).
(CIP Control No. : CIP2018032070)

The Power *of*
TODA(y)^2

By Jae Park

Get the most out of **TODAY**
For better tomorrows

To Dad

Thanks for asking me the hard questions

Special thanks to Noella Reeder,

Without you, this book would have never made it
out of my head and onto paper — and
it's turned out better than I could have imagined.

Table of Contents

The story behind this book

— My failure was catalyst in my success!

Hi, my name is Jae Park.

I wrote this book to give you hope. I want to encourage you to believe that anyone can have success when they put the right principles into practice.

I could begin like some motivational gurus do, and try to impress you with all the things I've accumulated, like nice houses and exotic cars, or tell you how many hundreds of millions of dollars of revenue the companies I run are generating, but in my opinion, that kind of focus isn't going to help you.

Instead, in this book, I want to tell you about some of my struggles and insecurities, and hopeless situations I've been in. I've come from a place that should not equate with the results I've achieved, but because of these strategies, I am where I am today.

If you're feeling discouraged or stuck, I want to let you know that you can still be successful even if you haven't had the best education, or think you don't have the opportunities and resources that others have.

Maybe you didn't graduate high school, make it into university, or graduate with the right honours, but that doesn't have to hold you back. If I can find success, so can you.

I have my own share of weaknesses and failures, and even a learning disability, but I've found a way to overcome them. As a matter of fact, the idea for this book was birthed at a time when I, and the management team for my family's company, were being reprimanded by my father for screwing up!

I've come a long way since then, and learned some valuable lessons. I appreciate you taking the time to check this out, and I hope this information will be as valuable to you as it has been to me.

Sincerely,

Jae Park

Introduction

How are you positioned for achieving the things you most desire? If you keep living the same way you have been, do you think things are really going to change? Do you find yourself regretting wasted time and missed opportunities? You're not alone! I used to feel that way too until I learned to harness the true power and potential of TODAY.

Maybe you're rocking it and reading this is just another step in your journey of self-development — if so, that's awesome! This book will help you take it to the next level! If you struggle to 'find the time' to do the things most important to you, and sometimes lose hope of turning the vision you have for your life into a reality, then you're also in the right place!

This book isn't a 'get-rich-quick fix'. It's an exploration of the power and potential of TODAY and how you can use it to achieve success in almost every area of your life. It's based on some simple, yet very powerful concepts, that can be used daily to keep you on track to reach your desired destination.

First, we will look at 'TODAY' and its importance to you. Then we'll break it down, using each letter of the word TODAY to help you remember the important mindsets and habits you need to form in order to get the most out of every day.

They are:

Time
Opportunity
Development
Assessment
Yield^2

(If you're wondering what that little 2 above the word Yield is, I explain it in the section on Yield — it's about power and has something to do with rapidly increasing the things you produce!)

When you put these six elements into practice in your life, something truly awesome starts to happen! Your dreams, plans, and goals come to life one step at a time, and when you use them all together, you'll see exponential growth and daily progress!

The Power of TODA(Y)^2 is not the 'end all-be all' book to take you to success! There are other things you need, but it is one of the key tools you should have in your 'tool-box'. This book is a primer. It's a daily reminder to help keep you on track. It's powerful enough, so that if you're off track, in just one day, you can change your direction. You can't change your life in a day, but you can change where its headed. The sails can be adjusted and your course can be set. If you've been facing hopelessness, despair and disaster, in just one day you can turn the wheel and face your dreams.

As long as you string more good days than bad days together, then you're going to get a positive result. Just like working out, there will be some cheat days. You're going to get a mulligan once in a while! But you have to perform better more days than not. You have to do your exercise more days than you're off. You can't work out one day a week and expect results!

I've learned that in order to really build the momentum

you need to create change, it's more like 5-6 days a week for a sustained period, like six months, with maybe having one day off.

When it comes to pursuing our dreams, we're conditioned to think, "Oh I'll work on my dreams from nine to five." You don't have to work twenty-four hours a day your whole life, but if you listen to a lot of people that have succeeded, there's a period of time that you have to work harder to get yourself out of a rut, or build momentum. It could be three months, six months, a year, or even three years, but it has to be enough time to get the ball rolling.

I don't want to give people the false hope that working on their dreams and opportunities from nine to five will probably lead to success. No, it takes a lot of hard work at the beginning, but it only has to be sustained for a certain period of time.

The strategies in this book will help you keep a good perspective on the main important things you want to accomplish. I use them regularly when I teach teams, and personally as well, to do course corrections on everything that I do. I don't know how **TODAY** worked out so perfectly as an acronym, but I would use it as a summary of what's worked for me so far. When I explain it to people, it just really rings true with them.

One, it's really simplistic and memorable. It's so complete, even though the parts are all different, but it doesn't work well if even one is missing. They all fit together to make a complete whole. It's a way of thinking that's really powerful. You can use it to judge what you did with your time today and ask yourself:

Time — "How did I use it?"
"Do I have the right attitude towards it?"

Opportunity — "What opportunities did I take advantage of today?"

It could be one of those times when you have a meeting with somebody and you really don't feel like going, but if your brain is primed, you'll think, "Maybe I don't feel like it, but it could be my opportunity. Maybe they will lead me to something that I really need, or maybe I have something they need!"

Development — "What did I do to challenge myself today?"
"What did I do to develop my relationships, business, personal growth, etc.?"

Assessment — "What can I change or tweak? What do I want to have in my life?"
Take the time to exercise your thinking 'muscles' to assess your life. You can say, "I'm the engineer, or coder of my life, so what can I do differently?" or, "I'm the baker, what ingredient am I going to change?"

Yield — "What tangible thing am I going to produce to-day?"

"How can I go from great intentions that are just living in my head, to making it happen step by step?" You actually have to roll up your sleeves, get out there and catch something to eat, or make something with your hands, to show tangible results at the end of the day.

Then the second part of **Yield** is to serve a higher purpose, something more than yourself. You can ask yourself, "What are my motives? Am I doing this for the benefit of others, or just myself?"

"How can I do more to serve others?"

Okay, if you're still with me, and interested in improving the quality of your tomorrows by using today wisely, then let's dig in!

We'll start with the story of my mistake that led to the writing of this book!

In the Beginning

The Disaster that Drove me to Succeed

In my preface, I mentioned that I didn't just want to focus on my successes, but rather, I wanted to share some of my weaknesses and failures, and how I overcame them, so I could give you hope.

Maybe you aren't where you want to be, and think you don't have the resources to get ahead in life. If you don't have a university education, or didn't graduate high school, that doesn't have to limit you.

I wasn't even accepted into business school, yet I'm currently experiencing success in multiple businesses! In university, I wasn't smart enough to get into the business faculty because my GPA wasn't acceptable. I was 'too stupid' to do business, so I wondered what else I could do. I looked at economics, but it was so boring, I couldn't stand it. I just took a bunch of electives instead, and after four years, I didn't even manage to graduate.

I wasn't great in school, but I'm a hard worker. My heritage is Korean, and though I was raised in Canada, my parents, who had their own business, instilled in me the work ethic Korea is famous for.

I was working for my father, managing his two retail shops, just squeaking by to make ends meet for my family, when I started to examine my life. I was thinking to myself, "I'm definitely hardworking, diligent, above average in terms of my intellect, education, and what I've been exposed to. I know that I'm smart enough, and I can work hard enough, but why don't my results show it? Why doesn't my bank account show what I know?! What am I missing?"

The problem I had, that many others share, was knowing I could produce so much more, yet the results in my life weren't equal to what I knew my potential was. Then the first catalyst that sparked the change I needed happened.

Catalyst: *an agent that provokes or speeds significant change or action*

— *Merriam Webster Dictionary*

I was introduced to a woman named Krista who invited me to look at an opportunity to build a business through an MLM company that sold protein shakes for weight-loss and building lean muscle. I accepted her invitation to check it out and found the product interesting, so I decided to go for it.

Prior to this, I had gone through traditional learning at school, university, and working at my family business, and learned many things, but as soon as I signed up for this, it sparked something in me! I got fired up, and all of a sudden, I was making over 100 phone calls per week, cold calling, going to meetings, parties, and events! Something in all of that really excited me! I enjoyed the extra income that came in, but the education I got from it was the most valuable to me.

If I didn't say 'yes' to the opportunity Krista offered me, or decide to hop on a call to see if there was anything that interested me, then I wouldn't have learned the invaluable skills that I use today — sales presentations, international sales, problem solving, leadership, and team building. I didn't pay for all these things I learned, but actually got paid to learn them.

I overcame fear and learned a lot by making so many sales presentations. I wasn't afraid to pick up the phone or start knocking on doors. I had one-on-one and group mentoring from millionaires, and got interested in personal development, reading many books on leadership, team building, and international sales.

In 3 years, I read over 350 books, and that's where my ideas started as I began to see patterns in many of these books. Well, I say that I 'read' all those books, but that's not really the case. You see, I have a type of reading disability.

I can't read very well. I can't read past 10 pages, or sometimes even 5. My brain just can't focus on words after a while, so I struggled all throughout university because I couldn't sit my butt down long enough to read very large chunks. Huge textbooks and chapters are impossible for me.

I have that weakness, but I found that I have a different strength which helps make up for it. I have the special gift of being able to retain over 80% of anything I listen to. Where most people can't retain more than 20-30% of what they listen to audibly, I can retain 80% and sustain that for about 3-5 hours. I can absorb a lot of information and still retain it even if it's sped up to 2x like you can do on your iPhone.

Instead of being frustrated with my inability to read, I used my 'superpower' and listened to many audio books while driving, or doing other tasks where I could listen. I couldn't excel in academia and get the grades I needed because of my learning disability with reading, but focusing on my strengths instead of my weaknesses helped me get ahead.

I was feeling pretty good about myself at this time. I felt on top of the world. I was seeing success in the new business, and I thought, "Now this has to be it!" I had my basic income working for my father, but now I had a side income that was growing into the thousands every month. It was very, very, significant when you've just barely been paying your bills.

In that first year, I became one of the fastest growing sales people in the company, earning an extra $50,000. Now I had some money in the bank — some disposable income. At that moment, I thought that everything I did would turn to gold, but then I fell into a scam!

I was contacted by an investing company that seemed to have some hot strategies. I invested $1000 to give it a try, and doubled my money, so I put in a few more thousand and it doubled too.

Everything seemed legit. The documents were very professional, and I even travelled to an office they had set up in Toronto, but then I made a costly mistake. I invested all my money, as well as a large line of credit, and wound up losing it all! I had been up 50K, now I was close to 80K in bad debt! I lost it all overnight. I was on top of the world, and now I was so low. After all my hard work that helped me get ahead, now I was way behind.

Also, at that time, my business with the MLM company I had been successful with was winding down. I just wasn't motivated to keep pushing like I'd been in the beginning, so that income stream was dying off.

I had to look my wife in the eye and hear her say "I told you so." She hadn't really believed the investments were legit. At that low point, I had to sell all the guitars I'd collected over 15 years, my extra car, anything I could liquidate, for basically pennies on the dollar, just to recoup a little of my losses. It took me 3 years to pay off the $80,000. That was about 1000 days of not eating out once, or even going to McDonald's when the kids pleaded with me.

It was a painful experience and a big hole I'd dug myself into, but believe it or not, that mistake was the second catalyst that lit a fire in me. That experience really made me grow and mature.

As Will Smith says in his famous motivational speech, "Fail early, fail often, and fail forward!" Well, I'd failed big time, but it had big positive results in the end! Out of my failure was birthed the question, "Now that I'm so far behind, how can I leverage myself and work harder and smarter?" Some of the answers to that question are the principles I've recorded in this book. They've helped me leverage my time and get ahead faster than I ever could have dreamed. In just a few years, I've gone from financial disaster to a steadily climbing success, yet it all started from the first questions I asked myself:

"What do I need to do to see better results with my potential?"

"What do I need to apply to get to where I want to be?"

Today, the results I am achieving personally and professionally are all based off of what I've learned through mentors, books, personal development, and the experiences of failure! This book, and the other things I teach, are all from personal experience and results.

So, enough about me! Let's look at the first section which will prime you to get the most out of this book.

It's Prime Time

preparing to get the most out of this book

Let's 'prime' ourselves a bit before we jump into the meat of this book.

The Power of TODAY^2 is about preparing yourself to get the most out of every day. Being properly 'primed', or prepared, makes a huge difference in your daily productivity. It's like the difference between digging with a shovel and wheelbarrow or using an excavator! It's all about the tools you use and knowing how to use them.

I included this section because it will help 'prime' you to get the most potential out of this book.

There are many definitions of the word prime — let's look at four of them.

The first: the best quality, or the choicest part of something, like prime real estate or a prime cut of beef.

We all desire the best in life — the 'prime' things. Using the information in this book can help you to attain those things.

The second: the most important, like a patient's health is of prime importance to a doctor.

The skills and topics in each section of TODA(Y)^2® are of primary importance to productivity and success.

The third: the beginning or earliest stage of any period, like primary school.

The concepts in this book are the first, or primary things that should be mastered on the road to success.

The fourth, (and main meaning for prime that this book is focused on): *to prepare or make something ready for a particular purpose or action*, like priming a pump by pouring liquid into it, putting fuel into a carburetor before starting an engine, or covering a surface with a coat of primer before painting.

You must prime yourself in every area we will be discussing, to prepare for true success.

If you've ever painted a house, you'll know the importance of priming the surface first. You have to fill in holes, sand, and apply a base coat before applying the final coats of paint that make it look its best. In order to have a beautiful life, you must do the priming first. It isn't the most fun, but it is the most necessary.

If you understand how pumps work, you will know the importance of priming them by adding a bit of fluid so they will run efficiently. Some of us are just go-go-go, but our engine is running dry and getting nowhere because we haven't primed ourselves before getting 'busy'.

Here's a sentence using all the forms of prime that explains why I created this information for you:

"To have a life full of prime things, it is of prime importance that you prime your mind, attitude, heart, and hands, to master these primary production behaviours!"

Now that you understand more about the word prime and why I use it, let's start by priming your mind to really absorb the information here and put it into practice.

The Four Definitions of "PRIME": Preparing Yourself to Get the Most out of Every Day

1. The best quality, or the choices part of something
2. The most important thing
3. The beginning or earliest stage of any period
4. To prepare or make something ready for a particular purpose or action

Priming Your Mind

———

If you can change your mind, you'll change your life. Changing your mind doesn't just happen from learning a new piece of knowledge. It happens by changing the way you think about something as well as actually changing your thought habits.

I'm not an expert, but there is an interesting piece of scripture in the Bible in Romans 12:2 that says we are 'transformed' by the renewing of our mind. The transformation on the outside comes from doing a 'mind renovation'.

You are going to be encouraged throughout the following sections to 'prime' yourself by preparing your mind to be open to some new ways of looking at things, especially in the area of opportunities that come your way.

Priming your mind is preparing your mind. It is the beginning, or primary step, towards actually changing your thoughts, attitudes and behaviours. It's like opening the door before you walk through. If you don't have an open mind, you can't get access to it to rearrange things.

This is obviously a big topic, but there is just one key area I want to focus on now. It's how you think about and see yourself and your current habits.

You might say, "Jae, I'm just a disorganized person! I don't know if this will work for me!", or maybe you see yourself as someone who starts things, but never seems to finish them. That's the problem. You will act as you identify yourself — so change your identity!

All of our habits, good or bad, came from somewhere — they had a beginning. We are just a product of our thoughts.

In T. Harv Eker's book *Secrets of The Millionaire Mind*, he describes the process of our thoughts: thoughts lead to feelings, which lead to actions, which equal results.

Carried further, he states that our thoughts come from our programming, so it would look like this:

Programming → Thoughts → Feelings → Actions = Results

You are not really who you think you are! You can repro-gram yourself, create some new habits, and look like an entirely different person with a different life in just a short while.

A Dramatic Change

———

There's a story about a guy that was mentoring a young man who had come to a standstill in his business. We'll call the mentor John and the guy struggling to grow his business Rick. Rick had reached a plateau and just couldn't seem to break through.

John talked with Rick and discovered he had many per-sonal fears and habits that were holding him back in his personal life that were affecting his business. In order to break past Rick's 'glass ceiling', John got him to do things that would break him out of his habits and fears.

Rick lived in a little place with hardly any furniture even though he had money for more. John got him to move to a nice place and buy furniture. Rick was afraid of cats, so John told him to get a cat. He even went so far as to tell Rick to stop being a vegan and eat some meat! Anything different that John could get him to do, he got him to change. In a short time, Rick saw huge growth in his business.

He changed his view of himself and it helped him change his business. He became a different dude with a different attitude, and that changed his circumstances. He said within a few months he saw himself as an entirely different person!

So, my encouragement to you before you begin this journey with me, is to prime your mind by opening the door to the idea that you aren't stuck being the same person with the same circumstances.

You are who you decide to be, depending on the new thoughts and habits you embrace.

The Secrets of Sports Superstars

———

Sports-stars are masters of these 5 'P' words: Prime, Perspective, Practice, Position, and Potential.

In sports there is a lot of training that goes on before the winning passes, catches and goals are scored. A player needs to be in the right position in order to catch the ball.

In order to be in the right position they need to train their perceptions to be hyper-aware of the players around them, the position of the ball and the anticipated moves of others. They also need to be primed and prepared through honing their skills with practice so they will be able to execute the right play at the right time.

Every athlete has the potential to be a winner. None of them will reach that potential without practicing the skills needed in their sport.

Athletes are a 'prime example' of people who know about the power of being prepared. They don't go to a game without priming themselves mentally and physically with practice. All their practice and preparing themselves puts them in position for a greater potential of winning.

We all have the potential to win in life. Whether we win or not depends on how we position ourselves. It depends on the perspective we develop and how aware we are of ourselves, and the people and opportunities around us. It depends on how well we've primed ourselves through practicing the right habits that lead to success — the habits that position us to live up to our potential.

> "Practicing the elements of this book will prime you and change your perspective so you can position yourself to live to your full potential!"

It's 'Prime Time' to prepare yourself to get the most out of today and every day!

That's where we're going to begin in our first section —

Today — The gift that keeps giving if you use it right

Another way we prime ourselves for true change is to stop and take action on the things we learn. Sometimes we can be so focused on learning a new concept that we don't take time to put it into practice. Each section will have some assignments for you to do. I encourage you to take the time to do them.

Assignment for this section:

Assignment for priming your mind: Practice being a different person

We 'see' ourselves as what we do. We define ourselves by our regular actions and responses. In this assignment, I want you to break out of the mold you've been in, by changing things up a little.

Think of three average things that you 'always' do. It can be the order you do something, the way you style your hair, the clothes you wear, the foods you always eat, etc.

Now practice doing some things differently. See if you can surprise those around you, or even better, if you can surprise yourself!

Today

The gift that keeps giving if you use it right

'Today is the first day of the rest of your life.'

It's important how we live today because it affects all our tomorrows. The moves we make today set up and position us for the goals we hope to achieve in the future.

All we have is today — this moment — now. The past can never be regained. The future is not assured, and the only way to touch it is by what we do today.

When naming this book, I debated whether to call it The Power of TODAY, or The Gift of TODAY. The fact is that TO-

DAY is a very powerful gift! Each and every day you have
the privilege of being alive on this planet is filled with infinite 'seed potential' and it all depends on how you 'plant
your minutes'.

We receive many gifts over our lifetimes. Some we use
well and others collect dust on the shelf or wind up in the
dump! The problem with the gift of today is that it has a
24-hour expiry date!

Many of us treat today like no big deal and put off important things until 'tomorrow', or another time, not realizing
that we might not have tomorrow, and that tomorrow will
never be different if we don't change today.

The good news is that you *can* change your life today.

You may not be able to get all the results you want today,
but you *can* make a change and 'set your sails' to get you
going in the right direction.

When your direction changes, then, you have hope.

You'll still need to build up some good habits and put in the work, but if you follow the principles in this book, you will see more success than most people ever achieve.

It's not a 'get rich quick' scheme, but an assessment tool that you can use every single day to help you make small necessary corrections, just like a sailor does to stay on course.

Many people think that they have to make a big change, and they don't see the power in making small adjustments in their life. The problem is that being 'off' by just a bit can make a big difference down the road. Darren Hardy uses a flying analogy to explain this. If you are flying from LA to New York but are off by half a degree when you leave, at destination you would be miles away from the airport! That's why the pilot makes course corrections all the time. If you don't make these course corrections every day, you could end up far off your goal.

I've had to use these course corrections in all different areas of my life.

Many Little Tweaks Create Perfection

———

A good example of my use of course corrections in business are the food products that we sell. We regularly get compliments and comments in our customer service department where people joke about how addictive our treats are and how they need an intervention to stop eating them!

How did we get our products to be so delicious and addictive? We tweak the recipe of every product we make an average of 200 to 300 times! We bake it hundreds of times, making small adjustments until it's just perfect! After that our product sells itself — one taste and people are sold on it!

I know that we wouldn't be as successful in selling them if we hadn't made every one of those small changes.

> **"We are what we repeatedly do. Excellence, then, is not an act but a habit."**
> — *Will Durant, American writer, historian, and philosopher*

One good productive day, turns into two, then three, and if you keep at it, it will build up to an amazing result.

In 2013, I was in a really bad financial situation.
A few years later, when I would share my story, people would ask, "How can that happen in just a few years?"
It can happen if you're just consistent every single day.
I had to correct the way I'd been doing things. I put into practice the things I was learning from successful people I looked up to. I focused on doing the things I needed to do every day that would get me to my goals. None of this is rocket science! As Stephen Covey says, "What is common

sense isn't common practice!"

People say, "It's just common sense," but the reason why they aren't getting the results they want is that everyone knows what they *should* do, but they just don't *do* it.

Dad Had to Knock Some Sense into Us

The story for how this book and my original idea for the TODA(Y)²® acronym began is very humbling.

I mentioned in the introduction that the idea for this book was birthed from a time when my father brought the management team of the family business into a room and gave us a reprimand!

I and my fellow team members messed up big time early on and that's why my dad balled us out and told us we had to use every day wisely!

He was saying "You guys aren't even executing common

sense! You know the answers but you aren't doing it!" He's the one that coined the phrase "Use every single day wisely!" When I was in that room, I penned the first words and acronym that would become the TODAY training.

> **"Use every single day wisely!"**
>
> — *Dad*

Many people learn a new concept, which might stir an emotional response, but then they just leave it in their brain and don't take action on it.

There's a principle I call 'Knowing to the power of H³'. It's a progression of knowledge that starts in your head, goes to your heart and then to your hands.

Out of those three progressional steps, a lot of people just leave it in their head, or maybe they allow it to create an emotion once a year around January 1st. Very seldom do they take it to the step where true change happens.

The place where the 'mining' happens that produces the gold, is when they go beyond thoughts and emotions to doing something about it. H to the power of 3, or H^3, when, Head, Heart and Hands all work together, is where the 'power' begins.

Knowing to the power of H^3 Principle

Knowing something in your mind is like getting a car. Letting it sink deep enough into your belief system to create an emotional response is like filling the tank with gas. You now have a vehicle with the potential to take you somewhere, but if you never get in, turn on the ignition, and step on the gas, you'll never get anywhere. You'll just stare at your beautiful car and feel proud that you have it, but it will never do what it was designed to do.

Knowledge can puff us up with pride. We think we're really

something because we know something. We will never really 'know' something until we know it by experience.

Doing something with our knowledge is the key that activates its power!

> **"Knowledge is potential power — <u>doing</u> activates that power!"**
>
> *— Jae Park*

Beware the Whirlpool of When...

There are stories of boats getting caught in a whirlpool and sucked under.

Putting things off until another time is like getting caught in a never-ending cycle of getting nowhere and watching your dreams drown into the deep, never to be seen again.

A lot of people fall into the trap of "Oh, I'll do it next year, or I'll do it when…"

"I'll start saving money *when* I make more money."

"I'll go back to school and finish my degree *when* I have more time."

"I'll improve my eating habits *when* the holiday season is over!"

"I'll travel *when* I retire."

Waiting till 'when' happens is a fallacy.

Why?

Because tomorrow is not a sure thing.

I've met so many people who thought that tomorrow was guaranteed, and then they died way too early from an accident, illness, or some other tragedy.

One of the deepest pains we've ever felt in our family business was the day when a young woman I'll call MJ, who worked with me, didn't show up for work. One of her colleagues used to pick her up at the sky-train station every morning for work, but when MJ didn't arrive at her normal time and didn't answer her phone, her friend who was already late for her shift left the station with an eerie feeling in her stomach.

Later that day we got the tragic news that MJ had been hit by a semi-truck and killed instantly while crossing the street.

Experiencing the tragic loss of such a young life with so much potential makes you realize the preciousness of every day we have. I don't want to take one day for granted or waste whatever gift of time I have. You just never know when it will run out.

Sometimes, waiting until some time in the future doesn't work because your circumstances change and you don't have the opportunity to do it anymore, or you just age and don't have the strength or energy to do it!

This fallacy of "I can do it when…" is the wrong type of thinking.

Anybody that's successful doesn't take a month, a year, or a decade to decide to take action, they do something towards it right away.

If it's worth doing, it's worth doing now.

I was asking some friends and team members for some ideas of an example I could add here to show how I act on things quickly, and Dave, my good friend and Operations Manager of our main family business laughingly said, "Jae does everything fast! Jae hires people because he just gets a feeling about it. When he feels like that person is special he makes the effort to build the relationship. Also, when he feels like the company needs somebody, he does it now rather than pondering on it too much. He always seizes the moment."

I cracked a joke about being the same when I have to fire somebody, then said we better not put that in the book! Everyone laughed, but Dave added, "Even when he has to fire them, it's better to do it now rather than dragging it out!" He's right. It's painful and hard to do, but still better than leaving the wrong person in an important position.

I said earlier that we tweak our products hundreds of times to get them perfect. That doesn't mean we take a long time to get them out into production!

Recently we had an opportunity to get a new product into a big distributor and we made the deal and had all the machines and factory in place before even having the recipe ready!

Some people wait too long for their ducks to be in a row before putting anything into motion. If it's worth doing, even if you aren't fully ready, just do something.

Sometimes you don't do things because you think you won't succeed. What if you knew you couldn't fail? A lot of the time we psyche ourselves out by saying "Aww, it'll never work out anyways..." so we just don't attempt it.

> "If it's worth doing, even if you aren't fully ready, just do something!"
>
> — *Jae Park*
>
> "Don't wait. The time will never be just right."
>
> — *Napoleon Hill, American self-help author best known for his book* **Think and Grow Rich**

Here's a story about a man who ran out of time to fulfil his life's wishes:

Distraction Kills

A young woman was sitting at the kitchen table at her brother's house going through an envelope of their father's that they found after he'd been killed in a car accident. The girl who hit him had been on her cell phone, so distracted she missed a red light.

One of the things they pulled out of the envelope was

some folded paper that had their father's scribbly handwriting on it. He'd written it on the day his daughter was born. It was his 'Bucket List' — a long list of things he wanted to do before he died. His daughter was now 29 and he had only done 5 of the things on the list before his death.

As they tearfully read through the list, joking about their dad's bad handwriting, the woman and her brother realized there were a few of his bucket list desires they had each fulfilled.

The young woman decided to do the rest of them in her father's honor. She also became an advocate for safe driving and informing people of the dangers of distraction.

It's a touching story but shows a sad fact that in almost 30 years that man had only done 5 things on his bucket list! He wasn't expecting to have his life cut short by a distracted driver. He thought he still had lots of time.

This story has two important messages: first — do the most important things first before you run out of time, and second — distraction is destructive.

Distraction causes us to 'kill time', which 'kills' dreams, and in an extreme case like this, actually kills! Don't let distraction keep you from focusing on the important things. Don't wait too long, because time won't wait for you.

Psalms 90:12 (ESV) says, "So teach us to number our days that we might get a heart of wisdom". If we want to be wise, we need to be more conscious of what we do with our time.

The two things that I want you to take away from the first part of this training are:

1. You have the ability to change your life, but the Power of TODAY is living in the moment.
2. If it's worth doing, it's worth doing NOW, because you might not have tomorrow.

I don't mean only live for today like the phrase YOLO — You Only Live Once — where you just party now like there's no tomorrow!

I mean do the right things now, so you have a better tomorrow, and leave a legacy for the tomorrows of others.

Embrace TODAY.

Receive TODAY like the gift that it is.

Open it wide and use it to its full potential!

> "The key is living in the gift that is today while doing things that will positively affect my tomorrows and the tomorrows of the people around me."
>
> — *Jae Park*
>
> "You're writing the story of your life one moment at a time."
>
> — *Doc Childre and Howard Martin,* **The HeartMath Solution**

Today can have infinite potential, but unfortunately it is limited by a finite measure — **Time**.

Each day only has a measurement of 24 hours.

Out of those 24 hours, only so many of them are available

for use because we have to sleep!

The first important element of TODAY that we're going to look at is Time.

Time can be your enemy or your friend depending on how you treat it.

Let's look at how we can develop a more rewarding relationship with Time.

Time

Your most precious commodity — How to get it 'on your side'

> "The right attitude towards time will determine how we approach and respond to every event and aspect of our lives."
>
> — *Jae Park*

> "Time is what we want most, but what we use worst."
>
> — *William Penn, English real estate entrepreneur, philosopher, and founder of the State of Pennsylvania*

Having a relationship with a non-entity like time might sound like a strange concept, but the reality is that we have a relationship with everything in our lives, from people and places, to things. For instance, some of us have an unhealthy relationship with food.

How we view something affects the type of relationship we have with it. If we see someone as an enemy, we'll treat them with hostility — if we think they're friendly, we'll be more warm and open to them. If we've had a bad experience with something, we will dislike or hate it, and have negative feelings towards it, whether it's a food, a person, or a place.

I've heard many people talk angrily about time, and even say they hate it! It seems like time is against them and they never have enough of it in a day to get what they want done. They view time as their enemy.

What do most of us want to do to our enemy? Kill them!

The statement 'I'm just killing time' shows the low value we have for it. The reality is that time is a gift. It can be your friend if you are willing to treat it with more respect and value.

We all have the gift of time. None of us knows how long

our gift will last, so we need to savour every moment we have.

Instead of being stuck living in the past, only living for today, or just hoping for a better future, the key is to be living in the gift that is today, doing the things that will positively affect our own tomorrows and those of the people around us.

Some people do more with a year than others do in a lifetime. Others complain that they have no time to do the things they want to do, yet they seem to have time to play games on the phone, watch T.V., interact on social media, and hug their pillow in the morning while they keep pressing snooze!

Someone sent me a link to a game for my phone and said "You've got to try this!" I said, "I don't have time for that!!!" The average person comes home from work, has dinner and puts the kids to bed, then stays up until midnight watching the late-night news or their favorite shows on T.V.

Me and some of my partners come home from our regular work, have dinner, put the kids to bed and then have meetings where we work on our dream projects from 9 to 12.

One of the guys at a recent brainstorming meeting for this book mentioned just how unconventional our evening meetings are. He said "I was telling someone that I was going to a business meeting at 9pm, and they said, "What?! You're going to a meeting now?!" It's like there's some unwritten rule that you're not supposed to have meetings past set 'business hours'!"

People often want to get together with me and pick my brain for business ideas or mentoring. I'll look at my schedule and say, "Okay, how about this Saturday morning at 5?" It's amazing how many of them aren't willing to get up at that time. I'm willing to share my valuable time with them by having an early breakfast meeting, but they aren't ready to do something uncomfortable to pursue their dreams.

We all have the same 24 hours in a day. What we each choose to do with them is what makes the difference.

> "Don't be fooled by the calendar. There are only as many days in the year as you make use of. One man gets only a week's value out of a year while another man gets a full year's value out of a week."
>
> — *Charles Richards PhD, licensed psychotherapist and author*

Time is a form of measurement, broken down into seasons, years, months, weeks, days, hours, minutes and seconds.

If you look at a tombstone, you will see that it has two dates on it — the date of the person's birth and the date of their death. Our lives are measured in time. Every minute takes us one step closer to that second date on our tombstone.

You could say that time is life. In a way, killing time is like slowly killing ourselves! It is throwing away a portion of our life!

On the other hand, using time wisely and productively earns us time in the future, and leaves a legacy.

> "Time = life; therefore, waste your time and waste your life, or master your time and master your life."
> — Alan Lakein, author on personal time management

We are using up our life as we use time. It is a commodity. Time is the most precious commodity on the planet. It is worth more than all the treasures of the world, because without it, none of those treasures can be enjoyed.

Time can't be bought, sold, or transferred. It can only be used and managed well to get the most out of it. Once a moment of time is gone, it can never be retrieved again — it's very finite. It only exists for the moment that it's there and you never know when you're going to run out of it.

One of the biggest mistakes a person can make is thinking

that they have lots of time. A vast majority of people in their latter years are filled with regret because they wasted the most precious thing they had on foolish things.

Have you ever gotten sucked into buying something expensive that wound up being useless, and you couldn't get your money back? Buyer's remorse is painful, but it's nothing compared with the anguish you feel at the end of your life when you realize you never fulfilled the dreams you had!

Another tragedy that can happen is when someone thinks they have many years left to do what they really want to, then have their lives end prematurely, like the man in our bucket list story. So many people wait until retirement to fulfill their dreams, only to get a serious illness!

That book they were finally going to write dies with them. That invention that would help make life easier or more enjoyable for others never gets created. That important thing they learned never gets passed on.

Some people have the motto 'Carpe diem', which basically means 'seize the day'. We must 'seize the day', or grab what moments we can before they slip away, because we can't hold onto them. We can't stop or create more time, but we can spend it on the most valuable activities.

To seize the precious moments we have, and squeeze the most out of them, we must figure out the things that have the most valuable impact for us at this time, and the future, and do them NOW!

One of the ways I've seized the day is in writing this book. I've had the idea for it for a while but I'm not good at writing. I don't consider myself an author. I didn't let that stop me from getting this book written though. I know the information in this book is too valuable not to share with others, so I made it happen.

I tried a few times to get help writing it but they didn't work out. I didn't give up and decided to give a writer I knew, Noella Reeder, an opportunity to try. She had never written a book for someone else, but I thought, "Let's give it a shot and see how it works." We clicked, and the book that had been in my mind for so long came to life!

If you have an idea but don't feel like you have the talent to bring it to life, don't let that stop you. 'Seize the day' and look for ways to make it happen!

The Power of Leverage

When I got Noella, who was better at writing than I am, to work with me in writing this book, I was using the power of leverage. I was leveraging someone else's talents and time, combined with my own, to fulfill my dream of writing a book.

I continually develop relationships with people who have strengths I lack, who can also benefit from my strengths, so together we can create something we'd never be able to do on our own.

We learn about the power of leverage in science. You can lift a heavy object using the leverage of a pole. The relationship between your own strength and the strength of the pole enables you to lift something beyond your own ability.

Using leverage in your life saves time and increases the amount you can do in a measure of time. One person building a house alone could take years, but with a team of skilled workers a house can be built in weeks.

Many people today pride themselves on being able to do everything themselves. Here in Canada, it's a very individualistic society. Sometimes as individuals we can forget the time-redeeming quality of working as a team.

If you have a dream to create something, take a moment to think if there's someone you can partner with to get it done better and faster.

> "The common man is not concerned about the passage of time; the man of talent is driven by it."
>
> — *Arthur Schopenhauer, German philosopher*

Let's not waste our precious time on useless things like too much social media, cute cat videos, T.V., gaming, or other junk.

It's okay to take a break and enjoy some down time, and it's great to stay connected with people, just as long as it's not taking up too much space in our lives so we don't have the room to fit in the things that are really worthwhile to us and others.

We have to act today because we really don't know whether we'll even have tomorrow. It may seem cliché, but what would you do if you knew you only had a short time to live?

Would you just hang out and watch T.V., or would you want to share some quality time with those you love? You might want to leave an important part of yourself behind for others to enjoy, like a song, invention, nugget of knowledge, or act of kindness that leaves the world a better place.

What we do with our time is like an investment. We can throw all our time away on frivolous activities, like how some people waste all their money and never save for important things like their retirement.

We have the power to choose what we invest our time in. If we look at our life and ask ourselves some questions, we can see what we've used our time for.

How are my relationships? Do I choose to make the time to connect with my spouse, kids, family and friends? How is my health? Do I make the time to exercise and cook proper meals?

How are my finances? Am I watching TV at night instead of working on that project that might help me get out of my dead-end-job and build my own business?

Every moment is a choice of what behaviour to invest our

time in. The results we have are a direct reflection of what we do with our time each day.

Some people sit around feeling jealous of others who've got something they don't have, like a fit body, a great relationship, or a successful business, but are they willing to make the same daily choices successful people make so they can get the same results?

It reminds me of an old children's story called *The Little Red Hen*. In the story the hen finds a grain of wheat and asks who will plant it and all the other barnyard animals say "Not me!", so she says, "Then I will!". The story repeats this process through the cutting, threshing, milling and baking of a loaf of bread. Each time she asks who is willing to do the work, they all say "Not me!" and she keeps saying, "Then I will!" In the end she asks "Who will eat it?" and they all answer "I will!", but she and her chicks eat it all up before the rest can have any! It wasn't fair of all the animals to make her do all the work and then expect her to share the bread!

We all want to eat the bread, but there are many investments of time and energy along the way to having that loaf of bread.

You can't get back money and time you've already spent. All you can do is try to spend the time you have now wisely on things that are really important to you so you can have good future benefits.

> "The key is in not spending time, but in investing it."
>
> — *Stephen R. Covey, American educator, businessman, and keynote speaker, author of* **The 7 Habits of Highly Effective People**
>
> "If you 'spend' too much time doing unprofitable things, you'll get 'no change'."
>
> — *Greg Reeder, Educator and public speaker*

What investments are you making with your time?

The good news is that small investments, made consistently over time, can really have big payoffs! Many of us make the mistake of waiting for large chunks of time to do some important things, instead of just doing a little bit each day.

We wait until we have more time to make a meaningful connection with our spouse, or to exercise, or even clean the house. The longer we wait, the worse things get.

If we would just commit to making small connections daily with our partner, doing 10–30 minutes of exercise instead of an hour, or cleaning one thing at a time, we wouldn't get so overwhelmed. If you wrote one page a day, in less than a year, you'd have written a book.

When you motivate yourself to do something that you don't feel like doing, by telling yourself you'll just do a little bit, Newtons Laws kick in. *'Every object will remain at rest unless compelled to change its state by an external force applied to it.'* In our case, we need the *internal* force of our will to get us moving, but once an object is in motion, it tends to stay in motion.

If you have a pile of dishes, and you're too tired to do them all, but tell yourself you'll just wash the glasses, once you get started, you usually finish them. Writing a whole book seems like a big task, but writing 500 words is doable. Making important, but small investments of time each day, into the things that matter to you, will help you reap a large harvest in the future.

When we start to do something every day it becomes a habit. It takes twenty-one days of doing something consistently to create a new habit. See if you can find a way to make yourself do the small, but important steps towards your goals, for twenty-one days in a row. It will hardwire your brain to that new habit.

We're looking at the Power of TODAY.

What is TODAY? It's Time.

Time is precious. It's a finite commodity that can't be bought, sold, traded or given. We also never know how much we have left. We don't know when it will run out.

Young or old, it doesn't matter, we need to make the most of our time before it's gone. We need to get time on our side, by valuing it, and treating it with the respect it deserves.

Our life is measured by time, but it's also measured by accomplishments and relationships. The true measure, or worth of a life, is the sum total of what you did with your time.

People are remembered most for the impact they had on the lives of others. Some have a negative impact. Some are kind of neutral, they just exist, and some are treasured as examples to live up to because of the legacy of love and service they've left behind.

We build these positive relationships and legacies by training ourselves to be prepared for the next element in TODAY — **Opportunity**.

The next section will teach you to see everything that

comes your way as a possible opportunity to help you reach your goals!

Here's an assignment to help you get Time working for you Today!

Assignment 1 **Put a higher value on your life.**

Bill Gates, Warren Buffet, and Mark Zuckerberg all make over thirty million dollars per day, which breaks down into more than one million dollars an hour, and over twenty thousand a minute. Imagine for a minute that your time was worth that kind of cash!

You never know, if you invest it right like they did, that could be a reality for you one day.

Keep track of some of the time you spend on unprofitable activities, like TV, or social media surfing. Tally up how much it just cost you if you make $1,000,000 an hour, or $20,000 a minute!

Assignment 2 **Make some investments**

Think of some things you really want, like a fitter body, a

deeper relationship with your spouse, a more comfortable retirement, or even better — an early retirement where your money is making money for you!

Now I want you to write down a list of 3 of the most important things you want to 'invest' your time into.

Once you've done that, think of one to three things you could do to work towards that goal.

For example, instead of making a goal of losing 10 lbs, make a goal of action steps, such as —

1. exchange some carb-heavy foods for vegetables
2. cut out high-calorie drinks like alcohol, pop and fancy coffees, and drink water instead
3. walk 30 minutes a day or do 10 minutes of High Intensity Interval Training which works even better!

Assignment 3 Invest in people

When I talked about the power of leverage, I showed how working together with others can leverage your time. Take a few minutes and think of the primary things you want to accomplish. Ask yourself if there is anyone you know who can help you work towards that vision. If there is no one, start looking. Write down any names that come to you. Also, you could put it out there on Facebook, or tell your friends that you're looking for someone with certain skills to help with something.

> "If you want to make good use of your time, you've got to know what's most important and then give it all you've got."
>
> — Lee Iacocca, famous American automobile executive

Opportunity

How to answer when it knocks

> "See the opportunity all around you, or not!"
>
> — *Jae Park*

If you've ever watched movies about spies, or people who are elite-trained operatives of some kind, you'll notice that they see everything as a potential tool to get out of a bad situation or defeat their enemy with. In a fight scene, almost anything can become a weapon.

In this section we will learn how to see everything around us as an opportunity to be used to win the battles of life!

If 'Today' is made up of Time, which is a finite commodity, that we can either spend or invest, then Opportunities are the vehicles we invest in that take us where we want to go. Just like other things we invest in, like stocks, bonds, mutual funds, businesses, and even people, some opportunities are riskier than others. If we want to get anywhere though, we will have to invest our time in many different opportunities.

An opportunity is a chance. Every day, in different ways, we choose to give something a chance. It might be giving someone a chance by going on a date or hiring a person to do a job. We might take a chance on trying a new type of food that we've never tasted before. It could wind up being our new favorite.

Opportunities that come our way are life taking a chance on us. Will we play along and take a chance on life by exploring the opportunities it presents?

Will we prove that we were worth the chance that was offered?

The Power of Respecting Opportunities

Some of us take opportunities for granted and don't make the best effort to use the opportunity well. My father is a man who proved himself worthy of the chance given to him when he came to Canada years ago.

In 1980 he came to Canada from South Korea with a wife, two sons and $350 in his pocket! That was the legal limit of money allowed to leave South Korea with at that time. With an unfamiliar culture and not being able to speak the language, my father looked for any jobs that could support a family of four.

One of those jobs was at a local bakery in Whitby, Ontario, where our family first settled. A successful businessman named Angelo had a chain of bakeries and his bakery in Whitby was one of his under-performing locations. With no real training or support, my father was hired to run the whole store himself.

What a huge chance Angelo took on my dad! What an opportunity was handed to him, even though the odds of success seemed stacked against him.

With his limited knowledge and grasp of English, he struggled through early morning production and then trying to sell the products during the day. Sometimes he would only sell a few loaves. He says it took him two years to figure out how to make and bake a whole wheat bread consistently!

He tells stories of going grocery shopping with the family during that time and he and my mother just looking at each other knowing that they didn't even have $20 in the bank. They couldn't even afford to buy the groceries.

He persisted though, and within 4 years, the bakery was

stabilized and running well. Angelo saw what a hard-working and trustworthy man my father was, and what a good investment he had made in giving him a chance by hiring him.

My father had done well with the opportunity given to him and his hard work earned him his next big opportunity.

Out of the blue, Angelo decided to help my father fulfill a dream that he had of moving to Vancouver! He told my dad that he was closing down a location in Northern Ontario, then told him to rent a container and remove all the equipment and ship it to B.C.

Angelo said, "Open a bakery in Vancouver with the equipment and pay me back when you are successful."

Within six months of opening, my father was able to pay him back! That is the power of using an opportunity well.

When someone decides to take a risk on you and offers you an opportunity, make them glad they did — the odds are that they will open another door of opportunity for you.

Angelo's generosity had a huge impact on my family! It opened the door to numerous other opportunities that have blessed us. We were able to expand on that first bakery and now run multiple factories, shipping products around the world!

I am a strong believer in offering opportunities to others. I make it my personal mission to give others opportunities. If I see someone with a gift, talent and vision that I can get behind, I love to use my resources to help them get ahead. It can be as simple as helping someone get a computer, to investing in a recording studio where they can start producing. It's paying someone that's just starting out to do a job instead of always looking for the 'best'. Sometimes it's inconvenient but often it reaps great rewards.

Having the opportunity to offer someone else an opportunity is the most rewarding opportunity you can have.

> "Look for the opportunities to help others be successful."
> — *Jae Park*

We talked about investing our time wisely and that opportunities are vehicles we put our investments of time into. To me, giving other people opportunities is the most important thing.

People can be one of the riskiest things to invest in, but the most rewarding.

The interesting thing though, is that the person you invest in is not always where your return comes from.

The Mysterious Law of Opportunity

One of my mentors once told me, "Jae, don't expect help from the people you give help to. Your help comes from other people." I was blown away at that!

I found that he's right. It's a success principle that when you help others, you don't expect help back from that person. Your help comes from another place. Normally we expect that the person we give to should reciprocate. For instance, if I give Dave some help, then I expect help back from Dave, but it doesn't happen like that. You give help to whoever you can and then others will help you.

> "Look for the opportunity to give because, once that value has been transferred, it comes back to you."
>
> — Jae Park

We should always have our eyes open to see the opportunities around us and receive them thankfully, but we also need to prime our self to look for the opportunity to give back, encourage, and add value to people.

In trying to become successful, many people just look for what they can get from someone else, or how that person can help them get ahead. True success comes when you also reach out and offer your hand to help others climb higher.

Sometimes, when you offer help to someone that you don't expect anything from, they surprise you. One of my family's biggest successes happened because of someone that went out of their way for me because I did something for them!

You Never Know
Where an Introduction Can Take You

———

My father had taken his opportunity of opening a bakery in the Vancouver area and doubled it. He had enough success to open a second store and a factory to produce the baked goods sold there.

He had also improved it by adding a deli section and offering other products like specialty goods catering to the many ethnic groups in our area. We dealt with many different distributors and had offers of numerous products come our way.

My father was in 'semi-retirement' and I was managing the stores when an opportunity for a bulk price on a certain raw ingredient came our way. I thought, "Hey, we could really do something with this!", and started to look for ways to produce and market our own product that could be available for a larger distribution than just our two stores.

Right around that time I met a guy who was interested in getting us to do some business with him. I figured I would help him out and buy some stuff from him to try and help him succeed, but didn't expect much else to happen from the relationship.

This guy was thankful and decided to show it by introducing me to someone he knew that could help us get our new product into a large distribution chain. He didn't just say "Hey, I'll introduce you to someone", then not follow through like some people do. He was persistent and worked really hard to get the two of us to meet.

It was kind of funny, because the other guy actually confessed a while after we finally met that he really didn't want to meet me at the time.

We were both in Toronto at the same time. He was only there for a few days and was visiting his elderly parents and certainly wasn't in the mood to meet with some stranger on a Sunday afternoon.

It was the persistence of the guy trying to get us to meet that finally made him feel obliged to do it. That meeting changed the course of my family's business and my life. I'm so thankful that he took the opportunity to meet me that day and for the determination of the man who introduced us.

Within 3 days we had our product in front of the distribution company and within a very short while, it was accepted and we were off and running. We now have had to open a couple new factories to keep up with production and have multiple products that we distribute.

To show thanks to the man that made the introduction for us, we now share a portion of our profits with him. That one introduction is making him a tidy sum each year. He tells me, "Jae, you don't have to do that!", but I believe it is one of the most important success principles to pay back and show appreciation to those who've helped you.

I was primed to give the first guy an opportunity to do some business with us. He was primed to pay back and give us an opportunity to improve our business. The third guy may not have been primed at the time, but he did it anyway, and look what happened!

Are you primed and ready to give and take advantage of some opportunities?

Opportunities Lead to More Opportunities

———

An interesting phenomenon about acting on opportunities is that every opportunity you act on almost always positions you for more opportunities to come your way! When you take a chance on an opportunity it can have a multiplication or 'snowball' effect where one keeps leading to another.

If I hadn't said yes to the opportunity to take a few minutes to look at the MLM protein shake company presentation, then said yes to giving it a try, I wouldn't have had the opportunity to learn the skills that have opened the doors to the opportunities I get now.

Sometimes you look at your life and wonder "How did I get here?" When you look back you can see the different opportunities that you took that made the way for each new one.

The reverse is also true. If you find yourself in a bad place you can sometimes look back to the opportunities you didn't take that led to you being where you are today.

> "Acting on opportunities positions you for more opportunities!"
>
> — Jae Park

Opportunities and Chances
Don't Last Long

———

The problem with opportunities is that they have a short shelf life. Often, if we don't grab them now, they'll be gone because someone else took them, or it's just too late. Sometimes we get a second chance, but often we don't.

"Life is like a 6-slice apple pie at a 12-guest dinner banquet. If you just sit back and wait for it to come to you, chances are, you're going to miss dessert."

— Donald L. Hicks, author of **Look into the stillness**

Don't Miss Your Ride

———

There's a true story about a young man who had been offered a ride to work by an older co-worker that lived down the road. He was told to be on a certain corner at a specific time and warned not to be even a second too late.

He was running a little late the next morning, and while he was walking, he saw his co-worker's car coming down the road. He ran towards the spot they were supposed to meet and to his shock the man kept driving even though he saw him!

The next morning and every morning after, he made sure

to be on that corner with plenty of time to spare.

Opportunities have a way of teaching us to be more respectful of their timeframe.

Many of us have missed important opportunities because we couldn't make up our mind, chose not to take the chance, or just plain waited too long.

A Father and His 4 Sons

———

There's an old story about a rich farmer who had four sons. He decided to give his land to the son who showed the most respect for the wealth he'd earned. He gave them each 5 grains of rice and told them that at the end of 5 years he would give his farm to the son who had valued those grains the most.

The first son didn't feel like hanging on to them for 5 years so threw them away and then tried to trick his father by just getting 5 more grains of rice to show his father when the 5 years were up.

The second son was hungry and ate the 5 grains of rice so had nothing to show his father at the end of 5 years.

The third son put the grains of rice in an ornate container and bowed before them, giving thanks for them every time he prayed to God.

The fourth son took them and planted them. He continued to plant the seeds that came from each harvest until he had a large piece of land cultivated with rice.

At the end of the 5 years the father gave his farm to the fourth son because he had shown the greatest respect for the handful of opportunity his father had given him. He didn't throw it away like the first brother. He didn't use it foolishly like the second brother just to satisfy a momentary desire. He didn't just do an outward show of honoring it by thanking God for it.

He proved he understood its value by using it for what it

was meant for. He planted it, tended it and caused it to grow exponentially.

His father could trust him to do the same with the land.

Luke 16:10 (NIV) says, 'Whoever can be trusted with very little can also be trusted with much'.

The more you recognize even small opportunities and use them well, the more you will get.

The Pain of Missed Opportunities

There are many stories of people who weren't in time to apply for their dream job, or let that 'perfect someone' know they cared about them, but some of the most painful are the people who didn't take up the offer to invest in something that became very profitable!

We've all heard of individuals or corporations that are

kicking themselves now because they didn't invest in certain companies or products when they had the chance:

- Anyone who said no to Ray Kroc and his first offer of buying one of his McDonalds franchises for around $1000
- Myspace CEO Chris deWolf who didn't buy Facebook for $75 million. It's now worth over $500 billion
- George Bell who thought Google wasn't worth $750,000! Google is now the world's most valuable brand, ranking higher than Apple
- The many publishers who rejected J.K. Rowling's Harry Potter book
- The man Walt Disney encouraged to buy the surrounding land where he was going to build Disneyland that thought he was crazy

And the list goes on....

Out of the many examples, two specific stories about

missed opportunities stand for me:

Kodak — Fear of Loss

———

Kodak used to have a 90% share of the American market for cameras and their equipment.

Even though an engineer that worked for Kodak was the first to develop the digital camera, they suppressed it because of fear of losing the success they already had selling all the film and paper products involved in picture development.

Netflix and Blockbuster — Pride and Lack of Foresight

———

You might remember Blockbuster Movie Rentals who

used to be on almost every corner until the digital age took over! They once had more than 9000 stores and over 60,000 employees.

Meanwhile, Netflix had been selling mail-order DVD's, and had the brilliant idea to stream them, and sell a subscription to their customers instead. They needed capital to fund their idea, and approached Blockbuster offering them the chance to buy their company for $50 million.

The heads at Blockbuster didn't understand the new boom of the internet, and pretty much laughed at this small company wanting so much. Now there isn't a Blockbuster store still standing, and Netflix has become a giant company worth more than $61 Billion!

The stories of these companies are examples of lack of foresight, ignoring opportunity for fear of losing what you've got, and pride blinding you to opportunity.

> "Our lives are defined by opportunities, even the ones we miss."
>
> — *Eric Roth, American screenwriter*

There are different reasons why we miss opportunities.

Sometimes it's fear of:

- trying something new
- letting something go
- losing something
- being uncomfortable or inconvenienced
- making a mistake
- choosing the wrong thing
- failure

I mentioned earlier that I have strengths and weaknesses. One of my strengths is that I'm a 'big-picture' guy. I can look and see the larger vision for things but I'm not great at details. That's why I surround myself with people that are better with details than me.

For instance, in the cowriting of this book, I also brought my friends into it by getting them to read the first drafts and give me suggestions. One of them told me when he got to this bullet list of fears he totally related to them.

Recently he and I have been on a wild ride in a new business venture from an opportunity that fell in our laps that was too big to ignore. He had to make some big choices and changes in his life in order to take a chance on the opportunity.

He said, "Jae, when you asked me to step out into this new opportunity, I felt every one of those things on the list! I'm a forty-year-old family man and I went through the uncertainty and fear of failure and the pain of letting something go and trying something new."

We're still waiting to see if he made the right choice, but I'm pretty sure he did. Maybe I'll let you know in my next book. Either way, I know he'd be kicking himself if he never tried.

He felt the fear and did it anyways! That's what bravery looks like. You need to be brave to embrace opportunity sometimes.

So many lives are filled with unfulfilled dreams and desires, untapped potential and missed opportunities, and that's such a waste.

> "If you ask people what they've always wanted to do, most people haven't done it. That breaks my heart."
>
> — *Angelina Jolie, actress, filmmaker, and humanitarian*
>
> "One can choose to go back toward safety or forward toward growth. Growth must be chosen again and again; fear must be overcome again and again."
>
> — *Abraham Maslow, American psychologist, best known for creating* **Maslow's hierarchy of needs**
>
> "Our biggest regrets are not for the things we have done but for the things we haven't done."
>
> — *Chad Michael Murray, American actor, spokesperson, writer*

Fear is a serious issue, but there are two other things that cause missed opportunities:

1. Unawareness

Some people are just not awake to the fact that opportunities are all around us all the time if we have '*eyes*' to see them.

They see others around them that are successful and think they 'just got lucky'.

As the saying goes 'The harder I work, the luckier I get'. It's not just hard work that makes people successful, but also taking advantage of the opportunities that come their way.

Some of us are 'colour blind' when it comes to the chances that pass our way every day. Our world looks grey and hopeless because we don't see the world the same way successful people do — full of opportunity everywhere you look — even in the negative things that happen.

Some people make lemonade out of lemons, and others just make a sour face!

Some of the hardest things that happen to us can be an opportunity for more personal growth and strengthening of our character. Will we learn to be overcomers or just stay small by being complainers that always make excuses?

Almost every famous person or hero we look up to is admired for the obstacles they had to overcome. There is no victory without a fight!

Every moment we're alive is an opportunity for something. When we stop ourselves from just going through the motions, we'll see that life itself is one giant opportunity.

We can see every encounter with someone as an opportunity to share something important with them. We can choose to put more into every moment we have by starting deeper conversations or being kinder and improving someone else's day.

We need to wake up to the reality that all of life is an opportunity for improving ourselves and the lives of those around us. The more we acknowledge this fact and start living like we believe it, the more success we'll see in every area of our lives.

> "Opportunity is all around you — you just need to train yourself to see it!"
>
> — *Jae Park*

Different Ways
People Have Discovered Opportunities

———

Creating new opportunities in existing industries:

Richard Branson, founder of The Virgin Group that controls more than 400 companies, is famous for looking at new ways to improve on things that already exist. He studies industries that have been around a long time, like airlines and mobile phones, and finds ways to make them more unique and interesting which caters to a different clientele. He rebrands things with a greater 'cool factor'.

Opportunities birthed out of need and problems:

Stella Ogiale, founder of Chesterfield Services Inc., a licensed home health care provider company, saw an opportunity in her own difficult circumstances. She had a hard time caring for her special needs child and realized the need for at-home health care services.

It's now an agency with over 1000 employees providing much-needed home health care to all kinds of people. It was started by a woman who saw an opportunity to help others that she only realized because of her own tough situation.

Mary Kay Ash, founder of Mary Kay Cosmetics, used the frustration she felt at continually being denied a promotion because she was a woman to inspire her to start her own business.

With her life savings of $5000 she started what was to become a cosmetics empire based on a model that gave other women an opportunity to build their own business. She took a negative experience based on discrimination and turned it into an opportunity for herself and thousands of other women.

Seeing opportunity where others only see garbage

'One man's trash is another man's treasure' is the perfect saying for Brian Scudamore, Founder and CEO of 1-800-Got-Junk, 'The world's largest junk removal service' franchise. One day he was sitting in a McDonald's drive-through behind an old truck full of household garbage when he saw the need for people who might not have the ability to get rid of their old unwanted stuff.

Brian, who may have started out just a 'junk man', is now a motivational speaker who shares his entrepreneurial success story and is a strong believer in the power of personal and professional development.

> "One person's problem can be another person's opportunity."
>
> — *Jae Park*

2. Lack of Preparation

Some of us recognize an opportunity when it presents itself but aren't ready and prepared to 'catch' it. If you want a big catch, you need to have your net ready and prepared so the fish don't slip through.

As I've said before, a big part of being prepared is 'priming' your mind. Priming is preparing. Even a pump needs to be primed before you run it so it will work.

We prime our mind by believing that life is offering us opportunities every day, and by saying to ourselves, "I'm going out there to catch as many 'opportunity points' as I can, because I value my time, and time is scarce, therefore I need to use my time wisely. I'm going to be open to that invitation to meet someone new, because you never know how that connection might affect my life, or how I might affect theirs."

We prime ourselves to catch the chances thrown our way by keeping ourselves open to receive them, and by practicing overcoming our fears and laziness.

Many times, we miss an opportunity because it comes at a time when we'd rather be sleeping in or lounging on the couch. It might come at a time when the weather isn't fun to go out in, or through a person we don't think much of.

We can even prime ourselves to see the chances that come disguised as problems. Sometimes our biggest problem can become our greatest victory! Nearly every great person has a 'before story' that spurred them on to success.

Keeping our mind primed helps us receive and extract every ounce of possibility, opportunity, and value out of every day. It's a mindset that needs to be developed. You don't know where the opportunities are, but if you're closeminded you'll miss out.

A Coincidental Opportunity

I was reading a story recently about a man who nearly missed a very profitable opportunity. He admitted that if his mind hadn't been open, he would have missed it.

He had a job, but wrote a blog in his spare time, using WordPress as his platform. He was having brunch with his girlfriend at a hotel when he saw a convention being set up and recognized the familiar logo for WordPress. He said to her, "You know what? I think that's WordPress over there."

She answered, "Wow, what a funny coincidence."

He kept looking over and thinking, "Yeah, interesting coincidence."

He almost got up and left after eating but decided to go

over and talk to them and tell them how much he loved using their tools for his blog. He talked with one of the guys, wound up getting his card, and decided to follow him on Twitter.

Three months later, the guy did a shout out that they were hiring, and he applied. He got the job and now works full time doing what he loves — blogging, and helping others learn how to do it too.

If he would have just chalked it up to coincidence and walked on by, he would have missed a valuable opportunity! Sometimes it's the smallest moments that lead to the biggest life-changing events.

He could have said to himself, "I'm not in the mood to talk to people I don't know right now." Not being 'in the mood' keeps us from many wonderful experiences.

Champions in sports, art, business, or any area of life, aren't ruled by moods or emotions. They use every moment and opportunity to grow or practice.

Set your mind so that it is 'turned-on to opportunity'. Choose to have an attitude of openness and enthusiasm for new things, and it will help you overcome momentary moods.

Successful people are 'turned-on' to opportunity at all times, even when others are turning off. Actually, when others are winding down can be the best time to 'fish' because no one else is!

For instance, the end of the year is a time that many are slowing down in business, spending money in the mall, and going into debt for things they don't even need.

At the end of the year I'm productive as heck. I'm ramping up, doing meetings, and planning for growth, where other people have taken the whole month off! I'm not heading into January just getting ready to start a new year, I'm already sprinting and speeding up when everyone's taking two weeks off!

In the new year, people are starting from a standstill.

They're fat from all the turkey! I love this time. Everyone else has written it off, but I find it's the best time for opportunities.

It's really about priming our brain to value time and keeping our eyes open for every opportunity. I'm so primed for opportunities that I see them everywhere, all the time! I jump on them and catch them before they get away!

At the brainstorming meeting for this book someone said "Hey Jae, what about an example of an opportunity you missed?" I answered with a laugh, "I don't miss any!" Of course, that's probably a bit of an exaggeration, but it's close. I've trained myself to see them and catch them.

Developing Your Opportunity Catching Muscles

Just like a pro baseball player practices so they can catch

the ball every time, you can practice and develop your 'opportunity catching muscles'. Becoming physically strong, and maintaining your strength, requires constantly putting your muscles under some form of resistance.

It takes certain character traits to recognize and take advantage of opportunity. Some of those traits are: thankfulness, curiosity, optimism, playfulness, clarity, risk taking, open-mindedness, responsibility, and generosity. Let's take a closer look at them and see how they can help you become a pro opportunity-catcher!

Muscle #1 — Thankfulness

Priming yourself to have an 'attitude of gratitude' helps you to see opportunities that others miss because all they 'see' is what they don't have.

There is a lot of complaining going on in this world and it never helped anybody. It won't make you happy and it doesn't bless the people you complain to. It won't position you to get ahead because it doesn't solve your problems. You only have a finite amount of time in your day, don't spend it on complaining.

Complaining is a habit most of us have fallen into. Even if we don't verbalize it, our thoughts can be filled with unspoken complaints. We complain because we want sympathy. We aren't willing to change if we just want sympathy rather than results! We need to look for solutions, not sympathy!

> "Complainers never win and winners never complain."
>
> — *Anonymous*

Unfortunately, being thankful doesn't always come naturally to us. We have to practice it. It's good to start and end your day thinking and speaking out things you are thankful for.

The more you train yourself to 'see' your blessings and

look for the good in your life, the more blessings you will discover you have. That will lead to you 'seeing' when good opportunities come your way.

When I was a kid having to work every morning and weekend in my family's store, I didn't feel thankful for it! Now I see that it helped me develop the good work ethic that I have today. It was a 'blessing in disguise' that I am now thankful for.

The other important thing about thankfulness and appreciation is to show it to those who have helped you in any way. Whether it's your teachers, parents, spouse or co-workers, always go out of your way to thank them or show them your appreciation when you can.

It's a success principle that often inspires the people who've helped you to want to help again sometime.

For instance, a while ago I called Krista, the lady who introduced me to the MLM protein shake company, where I learned some of the business skills I needed to know so I can do what I do today. I said "Hi Krista, do you remember when you invited me to join that company? You know, it was years ago, but I want to thank you for inviting me to be a part of that company."

She's not currently promoting it and I'm not either, but it was the catalyst, the jumpstart to my entrepreneurial juices. It was the opportunity I took that positioned me to be ready to take all the other big opportunities I've taken that got me to where I am today.

Start to practice thankfulness — feeling it and showing it. It will give you the eyes to see opportunity and open up more opportunities for you.

Muscle #2 — Curiosity

Work on becoming more curious. Children learn so much, so quickly, because they have an open mind and ask a lot of questions. They aren't afraid to ask questions even when it drives their parents crazy!

Start asking questions throughout your day, especially if you feel that an experience or circumstance seems unusual, coincidental, or interesting. Ask questions like:

"What is happening right now, and why?"

"What's interesting about this?"

"Could this help me achieve one of my goals?"

"What must I do next to take advantage of this opportunity?"

You can also see an opportunity for improving something by asking yourself how it might be improved. A curious mind takes something apart to see how it works, then wonders how it could be made to work better.

Become a detective that looks beyond the surface of how something appears at face-value. Practice becoming more curious about the world you live in and the way things are around you. You might see the opportunity to do something better. That's what inventors do.

Muscle #3 — Optimism

Staying optimistic is vital for recognizing opportunity, especially given the fact that behind every problem is an opportunity to grow, overcome, and create something.

Start speaking this affirmation to yourself — "Every problem also has an opportunity I can take advantage of."

When you have a problem, practice thinking or writing down ideas of something good you could do because of it. Practice spinning a positive slant to everything negative that comes your way and see if something sticks. It could be your next big idea or opportunity!

Optimism believes in miracles and doesn't say "It's impossible!" It sticks with an idea without giving up at the first sign of a problem. It says "How can we make it work?" instead of "It can't be done."

Pessimists shoot down dreams before they can ever be a reality. They aren't good at seeing opportunities. They only see problems.

Developing optimism means allowing yourself to dream and create instead of doubting and pulling everything apart. If you've failed at something before start to look at it as a learning experience and a stepping stone instead of a stumbling block.

Muscle #4 — Playfulness

Being willing to have fun and to be creative and playful, instead of always being serious, enables you to think outside of the box. Visionaries are like children. They don't follow the rules. They can make-believe and create a new world, see a castle in a cardboard box. Take time to play with new ideas and 'see' new opportunities in old situations.

Another valuable skill in being playful is to be okay with not always winning! Play with new ideas just to have fun. If you only look at a problem with the perspective that it needs fixing you can get frustrated. Frustration inhibits creativity. Try to be as outrageous as you can in looking at something from a different angle without the grown-up part of you shooting it down.

New toys and games are invented from looking for new ways to play.

Muscle #5 — Clarity

Take the time to get a clear picture of what you want. How are you going to recognize an opportunity if you don't know what you want?

Police study pictures of criminals faces so they can recognize them in a crowd full of people. Get a good image of your goals in your mind's eye so you can spot the opportunities that look like a piece of that picture when you see them.

Clarity is probably one of the biggest things you need in order to spot opportunities. It's like knowing the exact model of car you want. You start to see them everywhere once you are looking for that kind of car. When you know what you want you can then see it when it comes your way.

Make sure you take the time to think about what you really want in life so you'll know what opportunities fit with your big picture.

Muscle #6 — Risk-Taking

When an aspiring 12-year-old entrepreneur asked The Virgin Group's Founder, Richard Branson, what skills he used to become successful, he replied that they're the same ones he uses today — "…the art of delegation, risk-taking, surrounding yourself with a great team, and working on projects you really believe in."

Whether you practice risk-taking by making bold moves while playing cards with your friends, or stepping out to do new things, you need to increase your risk tolerance.

'Faint hearts never won fair ladies', nor have they ever created successful lives or multi-million-dollar businesses!

Remember, opportunities are chances. Chances involve risks. Risks have the power for much good, as well as bad. You won't grow without risking something, so exercise your risk-taking muscle well. Start small and work your way up like any weight-training regimen. As humans we like to stay safe and avoid the risk of change. We like to be comfortable, but nobody ever won big battles and had great victories by staying comfortable. They had to take the risk of trying out a new battle plan. Practice putting yourself into some uncomfortable situations and stepping out of your comfort-zone.

My parents took a big risk leaving their home country and coming to Canada, where nothing was familiar to them! I hate to think what our lives would be like now if they would have stayed in South Korea and never taken the chance on something risky, like a move to the other side of the globe!

What if the explorers never left home to find new lands? I

dare you to get off your butt and explore some new possibilities for your life! You'll never know what treasures you'll find until you take a risk!

Muscle #7 — Open-mindedness

Keep your mind open to new perspectives and ideas. If you get stuck always doing things in the same old way, the new trends will leave you in the dust! Kodak and Blockbuster showed us how dangerous it is to be close-minded to new ideas!

For fun, try changing small habits. Switch up the way you style your hair or put on your clothes. Try different genres of movies or books. Experiment.

Practice looking at things from someone else's perspective, and you might just see your next opportunity. Take a look at something from a new angle like, "What would a woman's view of this be? Or a child's?"

Take the time to look around and wonder what life is like

in someone else's shoes. Who knows, maybe you'll invent something that makes life easier for someone with a disability.

Being closeminded to trying new things blinds us to the opportunities for development around us. Having an open mind is like having open eyes!

Muscle #8 — Responsibility

Responsibility is the 'muscle' most of us don't really like to exercise or acknowledge! Sometimes we'd rather make excuses or blame things on others rather than ourselves for the opportunities we fail to take advantage of.

We can subconsciously be hoping for someone, or something, to rescue us from our problems and help us achieve our dreams. The reality is that only we are responsible for making them happen. It is each person's own responsibility to look for opportunities, act on them quickly, use them wisely, and offer them to others.

You need to practice reminding yourself that you alone are the one responsible for what you do with the opportunities all around you. No one else can do it for you. Only you can work at developing the opportunity catching muscles we've been talking about.

Muscle #9 — Generosity

"It is more blessed to give than receive."

— *Acts 20:35 NIV*

"Give and it will be given unto you. A good measure, pressed down, shaken together and running over will be poured into your lap. For with the measure you use will be measured to you."

— *Luke 6:38 NIV*

When it comes to opportunities, giving to others is a key to receiving more for yourself. The reality is that people like a generous person. They trust them and are more willing to give them opportunities.

Giving generously shows that you trust there is more than enough for everyone. It is a practical way to practice an abundance mindset. The more we give, the more we receive in all ways.

Being a giver puts us in the perfect position for opportunity. Many opportunities result from positive relationships and nothing creates more positive relationships than giving and serving others!

Here are some ways you can be generous in giving opportunities to others:

- Introduce them to people you know that might be a good relationship for them
- Make them aware of an opportunity you've heard of that would be a good fit for them
- Share your time, resources and knowledge with them

> *Developing Your Opportunity Catching Muscles*
>
> *Muscle 1.* Practicing 'thankfulness'
>
> *Muscle 2.* Working on becoming more 'curious'
>
> *Muscle 3.* Staying 'optimistic'
>
> *Muscle 4.* Being 'playful' with new ideas
>
> *Muscle 5.* Getting a 'clear' picture of your goal
>
> *Muscle 6.* Increasing your 'risk-taking'
>
> *Muscle 7.* Keeping your mind 'open' to new perspectives and ideas
>
> *Muscle 8.* Taking full 'responsibility' for what you do with the opportunities
>
> *Muscle 9.* Being 'generous' in giving opportunities to others

Knock and the Door Shall be Opened

We've talked about being ready when opportunity knocks on our door, but it's also important to go looking for opportunity and knocking on some doors yourself.

> "Ask and it will be given to you; seek and you will find; knock and the door will be opened to you."
>
> — *Matthew 7:7 NIV*

Many of us are waiting around for opportunity to come to us, but we also need to pursue it and do some asking, seeking and knocking ourselves. We need to actively pursue new opportunities and create our own.

If the things you want aren't coming your way, go looking for them. Ask others to help you find them. Don't be afraid to go out there and make things happen!

I had to pursue finding an author to help me write this book. No one came to me and said, "Hey Jae! You know that book you talked about wanting to write? I know what a busy guy you are, so I want to write it for you."

That would have been nice, but it didn't happen. I had to do some seeking, knocking on some doors and asking. I had to take some chances and even deal with some disappointments and frustrations when it didn't happen right away.

Don't forget that opportunity is a two-way relationship. It likes you to acknowledge it when it knocks on your door but it also likes you to pursue it too!

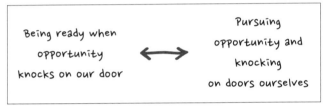

Opportunity is a Two-Way Relationship

We've talked about ways to develop opportunity catching muscles. Now we are going to go a little deeper and look at the importance of developing ourselves.

Just remember, we have TODAY.

We have a measure of Time.

We have Opportunities to invest our Time in.

The best way to ensure that our investment of time in the

opportunities we choose has a better chance of success, is

to work on the next part of TODAY — **Development**.

"To have more than you've got, become more than you are."

"Income seldom exceeds personal development."

— *Both quotes by Jim Rohn, American entrepreneur, author and motivational speaker*

Here's a few assignments for you to help you prime your mind for catching more opportunities in your net:

Assignment 1 **Practice overcoming mood and fear**

Think of things you know you need to do but don't feel like doing. Write down a few ideas of smaller ones.

Do one thing a day that you are uncomfortable doing, and keep yourself accountable by writing down, and keeping track of what it was, and how it made you feel after doing it.

Assignment 2 **Try fasting**

If you struggle with self-control over your moods and emotions, and have a hard time making yourself do the things you know you should do when you don't feel like it, I have an idea for you.

Practice regularly 'fasting' something. Fasting food is often done for health and spiritual reasons, but it is a wonderful discipline of controlling one of the most basic feelings we have — hunger.

Some people choose to fast one meal a day, or even one activity that they usually do, like watching TV.

I once heard of a guy who decided to fast saying anything negative for a number of days! It wasn't easy for him!

Assignment 3 Practice asking the right questions

Write out the questions from the section on Curiosity on a piece of paper that you keep with you, or make a note on your phone:

"What is happening right now, and why?"

"What's interesting about this?"

"Could this help me achieve one of my goals?"

"What must I do next to take advantage of this opportunity?"

When interesting things occur in your life, pull out these questions and think about them. Write down some answers and see where it leads you.

Development

The best time-saving device you'll ever invest in

"Personal development is a major time-saver. The better you become, the less time it takes you to achieve your goals."

— *Brian Tracy, Canadian-American motivational public speaker and self-development author*

"Investing in yourself is the best investment you will ever make. It will not only improve your life, it will improve the lives of all those around you."

— *Robin Sharma, Canadian writer and leadership speaker, best known for his **The Monk Who Sold His Ferrari** series*

In looking at the importance of using our time wisely, that

last quote is a good one to remember. Most of the time, we don't get where we want to go because we get in our own way.

Let's look at the definition of the word 'develop':

1. To bring out the capabilities or possibilities of, bring to a more advanced, mature or effective state

2. To cause to grow or expand

3. To bring into being, existence, or activity; generate, evolve

Every human is born with some capabilities and possibilities. It's what we do to develop them that makes the difference

Think about two farmers with the same seeds. One learns all he can about how to grow and protect his plants so he can have the biggest yield.

The other farmer just sticks his seeds in the ground and hopes for the best, yet feels jealous of the first farmer year after year because 'he just seems to have all the luck'. Maybe he even thinks God just likes the other guy more because he seems to 'bless' his crops!

Some of us have a hard time admitting or examining our faults and weaknesses.

Usually it's because someone else uses them against you, or it just doesn't feel good not being good at something, especially if others have ever teased, or put us down in the past.

The reality is that we are all a work in progress. The sooner we accept that, are humble enough to acknowledge the areas we need to grow in, and become hungry enough to change them, the better off we'll be.

Actually, being hungry can be a powerful motivator. Even companies that are leaders in their industry that stop being hungry to grow, change, and get ahead, often get overtaken by hungrier new start-ups that have nothing to lose and everything to gain.

Continuing to grow and develop is imperative to staying alive in business. Sometimes, companies refuse to change because of pride, like the Swiss watch companies that thought they were the best and didn't keep up with the trend of digital watches. Other times, companies can get too busy just trying to survive.

As individuals, we can fall into the same traps. We can let pride keep us from developing ourselves, or we can fall into survival mode. Something that keeps many of us from moving forward is thinking that we suck at something, so we avoid it instead of improving. Sometimes 'sucking' at something turns out to be an advantage!

I love this story I heard on the radio. I can't remember the name of the skier they were interviewing, but his story shows us the power of development even when we think we aren't 'naturally gifted'.

A young man had friends who loved to snow ski. He wanted to hang out with them, so he went skiing even though he was really bad at it compared to them. He got tired of 'holding them back', and being left behind or laughed at, so he decided to take some lessons so he could keep up.

That young man went on to become an international ski champion!

He loved the lessons and felt so good about the improvements he was seeing, that he went on to far surpass his friends!

> "There is nothing noble in being superior to your fellow man; true nobility is being superior to your former self."
> — *Ernest Hemingway, American novelist and journalist*

We should all be on the road to becoming a better model than our old self. If iPhones stayed the same, people wouldn't be such fans. A successful company keeps improving and growing in their products or service, and a person who wants a successful life should be doing the same.

You're either growing or dying!

To keep with the farming theme earlier, I think it was Jim Rohn who said, "You're either green and growing, or red, ripe, and dying!" It doesn't matter what aspect of life you look at, physically, spiritually, mentally, relationally, or financially, it is not good to try to remain in 'maintenance mode'.

If you're not pressing forward, you're slipping backwards. There are only two directions — forwards or backwards, growing or dying! If you feel like you've finally 'arrived', you're wrong! There is always more to learn, more to grow, more to improve!

Pride and arrogance in thinking you know it all, or the unwillingness to have a teachable attitude, will keep you from the opportunity of climbing higher than you ever dreamed!

Sometimes someone who is totally new to a situation can teach us something because they see it with different eyes!

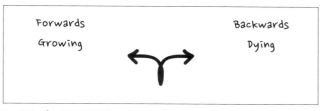

If You're Not Pressing Forward, You're Slipping Backwards!

I've talked about priming our brain to be prepared to see and act on opportunities. Well, we also need to prime our brain to grow, receive, and push ourselves in all the areas we can. Asking, "What can I change? What areas can I grow in today?" is priming ourselves for real change.

It will push us to develop — to bring things into existence in, and through ourselves that never existed before! It will cause us to mature and be more effective, leading to more and more advancement in all areas of our life!

> "Growth is the great separator between those who suc-
> ceed and those who do not. When I see a person begin-
> ning to separate themselves from the pack, it's almost
> always due to personal growth."
>
> — *John C. Maxwell, American author, speaker, and pastor,*
> *specializing in Leadership Development*

Personal growth isn't easy. It's not without some pain. Years ago, I joined a CrossFit gym and had been going and working out hard for weeks.

Every day my body was hurting, so I asked the owner that was a lead trainer there, "Hey, I've been doing this every day for weeks now, and every day my body aches. When does your body get used to it?"

He said, "If you're doing it right, it never should."

It's not what we really want to hear, right?

We don't like to hear that we always have to push a little harder, overcome a little more, and have some new grow-ing pains, but that's what life and growth are all about! "No pain, no gain!"

The fact is there are some things you just have to do your-self no matter how rich and successful you become. You can't pay anybody to do your push-ups for you. You can pay a trainer to help you do it right, or to motivate you, but you have to do the actual work to see the change that you want.

My Own Personal Pain That Led to Gain

Sometimes it's the things in life that seem the most dif-ficult that have the biggest influence on your personal development. When I think about a part of my life that seemed hard and painful at the time, but caused me to grow, I think about my childhood.

I told you about how hard my dad worked at the opportu-nity given to him at the first bakery job he got in Canada, then the bakery of his own he was able to open. Well, the bakery in Vancouver was a family business, which meant my mom, my brother, and I, worked pretty hard too.

My childhood wasn't very easy. My father is a very strict person. His training is very military-based. I worked every morning before school. You'd think that there's not much time, but there are a lot of hours before school starts! Going to school was taking a break for me. It was a walk in the park compared to chores at home and working in the family business.

I hated Saturdays because I had to be there a full day from 6am to 3pm, and working in the store was much harder than fooling around in class. I never got to be like my friends who would be able to sleep in on Saturdays and watch cartoons. I also hated summer and winter break because I had to work then too.

So, that being said, even though I gave up a lot during my childhood, I'm so thankful for it now because it taught me how to be a hard worker. While my buddies were filling their heads with cartoons, I was learning skills that would help me get to where I am today.

The pain of training and discipline is small compared to regret. As Jim Rohn says, "The pain of discipline weighs ounces where the pain of regret weighs tons." A lot of people can't give up small things for their big dreams.

You have the choice of either the pain of training yourself or living with what you have. If you're happy with what you've got, that's fine, but if you want more, then you have to put in more. Development happens over time.

The prime example is a fit person. You can't fake fitness, right? You can't pay somebody to do your workouts for you. It's the same thing with development — you've got to go through the pain of training and discipline to reap the results.

My childhood might seem like it was pretty screwed-up, but it gave me an unbreakable mindset that if I went through that, I can go through anything! If I could get up and work hard as a kid, I can do it now.

It's really about putting things into perspective. I was talking with someone about how things are all relative. For instance, when you say something's hard, then hard relative to what? Hard compared to not having shoes, or trying to get one meal a week in a developing country? Get with it, guys! You haven't been through that! You haven't been through a civil war, or genocide, like the Jews being persecuted in Germany! Life is often unfair to our advantage. If you were born in Canada or the US, or another prosperous place, you've probably already won the lottery!

Some of the strongest and most beautiful things are born from adversity. Even a lump of coal becomes a diamond because of the intense pressure placed on it.

> "You cannot dream yourself into a character; you must hammer and forge yourself one."
>
> — *Henry David Thoreau, American essayist, poet, philosopher*

> "Change equals self-improvement. Push yourself to places you haven't been before."
>
> — *Pat Summitt, American women's college basketball head coach*

Don't Just Develop One Muscle

When it comes to developing your muscles when working out, you don't want to just strengthen one muscle group. For instance, you need to do some push and pull exercises to work both your chest and your back. You don't want to have one area of your body weaker than the rest. If you want to lift a lot of weight you don't just need strong arms, you also need a strong back and legs. You can't lift much if one area is weak. They all need to work together.

Some of us are strong in one area of our lives, but weak in others. If you are physically fit, but spiritually weak, your life will be out of balance.

When looking at personal development, make sure you work on all aspects of yourself. You might achieve success because you have a good work ethic, but then have a hard time holding onto it due to poor relationship skills.

It's important to look at the whole picture when thinking of personal development. We can get stuck being focused on the outward things in our life when it's the inward things that play the biggest part of what we can achieve outwardly.

Personally, my outer world has only grown in proportion to my inner growth mentally and spiritually. I needed to be able to think bigger, and give in a bigger way, in order to create more growth in my finances.

Even in the food business I'm involved in, we don't only focus on one product. What if something happens to the key ingredient of that product? It's not good to have all your eggs in one basket. We are continually at work developing new products so we can be diversified.

There's a book called *Multiple Streams of Income — How to Generate a Lifetime of Unlimited Wealth* by Robert G. Allen. In it he shares stories of a few of his huge streams of income that dried up because of different disasters. He teaches that to have true financial strength, you should have many different income streams. If one form of your income stops, you will still be able to survive because of the others.

If you develop your inner self, it will help carry you when other areas in your life go through a rough time.

Strengthening Your Core

Keeping with the theme of muscles, having a strong core

is the foundation for all your other lifting. If your core is weak, you are at risk of hurting yourself trying to build your other muscles.

Just like it's important to start with a strong foundation when building a house, the best place for a person to start working is on their heart and mind. Even in fitness, priming yourself to have a good mindset before working out is the first key to a successful training session.

I can't emphasize it enough that working on your inner self should be your first priority if you want to see real results in the more tangible areas of your life.

Whether you're developing a fit body, a business, a relationship, a musical piece, or a recipe, somewhere along the line you need to stop and assess how it's going.

Where does it need tweaking?

Does something need to be added, taken away, or changed?

That's the next part of getting the most out of TODAY —
Assessment.

We'll look at how to make sure your investments into Time, Opportunities, and Development are being optimized for the best Yield.

Assignments for Developing your best you yet:

Assignment 1 **Grow Yourself!**

Think of the areas you most want to develop in yourself.

You may need to do some soul-searching for this.

If you brainstorm and write down some of the problems

you're having in life, either financially or relationally, with

your health, or abilities, you'll find your answer.

Too often when we have a problem, we think it's because

of someone or something else, and if they would change,

then we'd be ok. That's seldom the issue. When we change

ourselves, circumstances and situations don't have the

same effect on us!

Choose some of the most important issues and search for

some help. Find some books or online articles with tips

you can use to help you learn and grow. Read at least one

article a day and start putting some things into practice.

Remember — the magic's in the *doing*, not in the knowing!

Assignment 2 Ask Yourself the Right Questions

Always remember that your brain works best when it's asked a question. It's programmed to respond to the stimulus of a question.

If you are setting goals for yourself to achieve in personal growth, it is good to have your goal in mind, then work backwards by asking yourself specific questions.

For instance, "What are 3 things I can do today to get closer to my goal?"

You may have a goal of creating a deeper relationship with someone. You might not be able to guarantee that, but you can do things to make it more probable by developing your relationship skills and habits.

I could ask myself "What are 3 things I can do this week to be a better husband and get closer with my wife?"

My answers might be:

1. I can make time to have more intimate conversations with her, and ask how she's feeling about our rela-

tionship, and what she might like more of

2. I can make sure to give her a heartfelt hug and kiss before I leave for work and when I see her again at the end of the day

3. I can do something special for her by buying her flowers, or a little something to show I was thinking of her

Figure out an area you want to grow in and ask yourself the right questions. Your brain will likely give you the 'assignments' you need.

Assessment

The most life-changing chapter in this book

"The unexamined life is not worth living."

— Socrates, classical Greek philosopher

"It takes courage...to endure the sharp pains of self discovery rather than choose to take the dull pain of unconsciousness that would last the rest of our lives."

— Marianne Williamson, American spiritual teacher, author and lecturer

Assessment is probably the single most powerful chapter of this book.

If you don't know where you are, you won't know how to change to get where you want to go.

Each other part of the book is important, but what is ultimately going to make the biggest difference in getting you where you want to be?

Development's not going to do it. Your attitude towards time's not going to do it. Opportunity's not going to do it. Assessment is. You'll be able to set your direction from this chapter. Don't skip it, whatever you do! Assessment can be a powerful tool if people use it well and practically.

It might be hard for me to admit it, but this is what my father is really good at! He thinks through stuff and comes up with solutions that work!

I was challenged to write this book largely because of this chapter — because of thinking, coming up with solutions, problem-solving, finding options and analyzing. This chapter is where the power for real change begins. When I said earlier that we may not completely change our life in a single day, but that we can change and set a new direction in a day — this chapter is where that power comes from.

Assessment is life's most important navigation tool. It's like a compass that shows if you're on course or not, a tool that you can use to take you where you need to go. To assess something is to evaluate the quality or ability of it.

One of the powers that humans have that sets us apart from all other creatures, is the ability to reflect and examine our lives, and make corrections on our behaviour. We can reason, unlike animals, who just react and act on instinct.

It isn't always pleasant to examine our life, and the results of our actions, or lack of action, but it is vitally important.

If we never stop and assess our outcomes, we'll usually fall into the trap of insanity. We do the same thing expecting different results, and that's just plain crazy!

> **"Insanity is doing the same thing over and over again and expecting different results."**
>
> *— attributed to Albert Einstein*

If something's not working, then we have the ability to just take a step back and think, "Huh! You know what? Maybe I can just change the input. Maybe the order needs to be different. Maybe I should try something else. Maybe I should do something else or go somewhere else."

If the things that you've been doing have not been working, you have the power to assess and make changes. You can make course adjustments — once a minute, once an hour, even once a day, but it has to happen.

Living our life is like sailing a boat; we really need to make finetuned adjustments every day so we don't find ourselves far off course.

If you don't stop to assess where you are, even if you seem to be just a little off course, it can cause big problems in the future. If a ship or a plane is travelling a far distance and is off by just a few degrees when it leaves, it will wind up far from it's intended destination. Sailors and pilots are trained to continually assess where they're at so they know how much they need to adjust to get where they're going. It's impossible to readjust if you don't know where you are now and how far off you are from your goal.

It's important to assess. People are going through their day checking emails 80% of the time. They're busy doing non-important work.

As a matter of fact, one of the key members of my team told me that's exactly what he was doing for many years before he started working with me. He tried to prioritize but found himself busy just catching up on emails.

He said, "I was in a panic mode just busy doing too many things, and even lacking sleep, but Jae taught me to assess my work every day. He told me about the Time Management Grid from the book *The 7 Habits of Highly Effective People* by Stephen Covey. You write down all the things you need to do on a paper broken into 4 Quadrants. Quadrant 1 is Urgent-Important, 2 is Not Urgent-Important, 3 is Urgent-Not Important and 4 is Not Urgent-Not

Important.

I started to do an assessment everyday using this grid. I always checked that I was doing Quadrants 1 and 2 and eliminating 3 and 4. I try to do this every day.

After practicing that, now I have 500-600 unread emails but that doesn't distract me much. Not as much as before. I try to get things done that are important first and now my projects are actually moving forward!"

Urgent-Important	Not Urgent-Important
Urgent-Not Important	Not Urgent-Not Important

Stephen Covey's Time Management Grid

Its not always easy to say no to the distractions that seem important, but it is necessary. Taking time to analyse and decide which activities are the most rewarding, important, and truly urgent, is a valuable assessment activity.

Avoiding the Devil's Vortex

Using a quadrant-style assessment tool has been used by many different people in different ways. Author and speaker Darren Hardy attributes an increase in his success after using something called a 'Sunday Planning System'.

He met an older Catholic multibillionaire who used it all the time. Every Sunday, before his week began, he got a piece of paper and wrote his 'Divine Purpose or Mission' at the top. Then he drew a cross underneath as his quadrant. The first 3 squares were his top 3 goals — goal 1, goal 2 and goal 3. The last square he called The Devil's Vortex! As he thought of all the things that he needed to do to complete each goal, like phone calls or tasks, he would place them in the square with the goal they were a part of. If he thought of things that didn't fit in his 3 top priorities he would place them in The Devil's Vortex.

When we get caught up in the many busy tasks that eat up our time but don't get us to our goals, it's like being sucked into the Devil's Vortex.

However you do it, planning out your week before it begins is a good habit that makes assessing easier. You can look at your plan and assess whether you're on track or not.

Divine Purpose or Mission:	
Goal 1:	Goal 2:
Goal 3:	Devil's vortex:

Darren Hardy's Sunday Planning System

The Power of Checking Your List

Another tool some people use is a checklist.

In one of our stores, one of the new managers came in and saw that important things weren't getting done and that the shift leaders were having to remind people too often to do certain things. She decided to make up checklists in every department for each shift with the particular activities and times they should be done by.

It was a handy tool for new hires as well as a good reminder for the regular staff. It also took a load off of the management. They didn't have to be on everyone's case all the time.

One of the women working there found the checklists so helpful, she decided to write some checklists for the different areas of her personal life and things she wanted to get done each day. It was a physical copy that she could look at to assess whether she was meeting her daily goals.

Some people love the power of writing that checkmark and seeing a visible reminder of what they've accomplished. This might work for you.

The List	check
•	
•	
•	
•	
•	
•	
•	
•	
•	
•	

Checklist

Become a Better Thinker

If what you're doing isn't causing success, then the easiest thing to do is to find someone who's getting the results that you want and ask them how they did it. What are their habits and thought processes? Start thinking on their level and doing what they do!

We have the great ability to 'think' but we often take it for granted and don't use it. Maybe it's because we're lazy and trying to create something takes effort, because we naturally want to avoid work and go on the path of least resistance.

Sometimes I go to companies that take five steps to do something when it can be done in one, and their excuse is, "Oh, we've always done it like this. We've done it for 20 years."

Sometimes we don't try to think of new solutions to get us ahead because we're lazy or stuck in doing something the way we've always done, but it can also be because we're used to making excuses. We see a little roadblock in our way and we just give up and say, "I can't do it because..."

In my life, I don't want to accept the reason "I can't, because..." I'd rather say "Let's find the reasons why we can do it!" I don't want to get stuck in small thinking.

There's a ton of examples of this in all my businesses. My team and I are often very unconventional in finding solutions to our problems, not just for the sake of being unconventional, but sometimes because we don't have money or resources. Sometimes even money doesn't give you the right answer. You have to come back to common sense and using your brain.

What Looks Like the Right Way
Isn't Always the Best Way

———

Here's a story about a big decision I made using my reasoning abilities.

I live in the Vancouver area, and one of the things it's famous for is high housing prices. I wanted to get a bigger home that was more comfortable for my family and it seemed like my best bet was to buy land in a cheaper area and build my own house.

After doing research on land, I realized that even in the cheap part of town I was looking at about a million dollars, so I calculated what the land would cost, plus the amount to build the house, the time it would take me, and realized it wasn't going to save me the money I thought. I had in my mind that I was going to save $250,000 to $400,000 by building it myself, but that wasn't true.

It turned out that buying a house was actually cheaper

than buying a piece of land, holding it for a year, building, etc., so that's when I decided to buy a house instead of building my own.

The Power of Asking the Right Questions

You might be thinking, "Okay Jae, you're telling me to assess and use my brain, but how do I do it?" Obviously, you use your brain every day to do the things you do. I'm talking about taking your thought processes to a higher level.

Remember when I talked about the first inspiration for this book happening at a board meeting where my father was reprimanding us? Well, he didn't just yell at us and tell us everything we were doing wrong, he asked us some good questions.

Those questions provoked our brains to kick out of auto-pilot and really think about how to solve things! He asked good questions, and he asked hard questions, and those questions led us to come up with the answers we needed to get things running the right way.

Most of us go through life living on the surface. We ask surface questions like "How are you today?", which gets a surface answer of, "Fine, thank you."

We need to start asking ourselves and others the questions that go for the jugular!

I don't mean in a cruel way like "What were you thinking when you got that haircut, dude?" What I mean is like when your friend's complaining about his marriage, and instead of just saying, "That's women for ya!", you ask him, "What things can *you* do to make it better? What attitudes of your own can you improve to be a better husband?"

We've got to stop asking questions on the fringe and start asking something that will directly impact our direction and decisions today!

Think about the importance of asking the right question when you do a Google Keyword search. Everybody searches, but the key factor of Google searching is formulating the right words in the right combination. If you want to find out the right information and get better results on Google, you need to learn how to ask the right questions!

Dad's Company Assessment Questions

At the factory my father taught us some simple yet powerful assessment questions to use. He said, "Go to the factory, close your eyes and take in the atmosphere in the room. What do you feel? How do you see people working? If you look at a worker, ask yourself, "If that was my wife working, would she be comfortable?"

I now try to use that in every scenario. If I see someone working uncomfortably, I think, if that was my wife work-

187

ing, would she not want to work there? Quality of work is a key in our business. We want to make sure that people are working well and comfortably, so that's an assessment guideline for us.

If I was going to use one key phrase that sums up the most important skill in learning how to think on a higher level and assess your life well, it's this:

Ask better questions to get better answers!

> "Successful people ask better questions, and as a result, they get better answers."
>
> — *Tony Robbins, American author, entrepreneur, philanthropist and life coach*

The brain is a natural question answerer, that's how it works. It will just coast on default mode of running all the programs until you give it a problem to solve by asking a question.

I talked earlier about companies that keep doing things the same way because that's always the way they've done it. We might need to ask ourselves why we've done things a certain way, and then look if that reason still fits our life now.

Wasting the Roast

There's a crazy story about a woman who kept cutting the ends off of her roast before baking it, then one day her husband asked her why she did it. She said because her mom did it that way, so she asked her mom why she did it. Her mom said it was because her mother had done it, so she asked her mother why she always cut the ends off the roast before cooking it. The older woman said, "I did it because my pan was too small!"

Are you still doing things small because your thinking is

too small? Then ask some bigger questions!

Another reason to ask questions is because you might get a different answer than you assumed. Don't judge too quickly and think you already have the answers.

I was recently talking to an Indian man and asked him if he'd ever been to church. I thought he probably hadn't been, and judged him to be Hindu or Sikh. He said, "Oh yeah, I go to church regularly. I'm a Baptist." I felt bad for judging on outward appearances. Questions help us to go deeper than knowing something or someone on a surface level.

You might think your spouse is happy with you because they don't yell at you. But maybe they are upset about some things but not showing it! It can help to ask "What is something I could do more of to make you feel happier in our relationship?", or ask your employees, "What are the biggest problems you are having in your job?"

What I'm trying to say is, keep an open mind when you ask questions of others or yourself. Let go of the prejudice that you have, of what you think you know, and be willing to listen and learn.

Let's look at some tips on asking the right questions.

The Power of the 5 W's

———

Journalists are taught to answer the 5 W's when they write news articles. People want answers to who, what, where, when, why, (and how). They will even write those words down on a page, then do the research and ask the questions to fill in those answers.

Who, what, where, when, why, and how are the best thought-provoking questions to start with in solving problems, or searching for answers. This might seem too simple, but often the simple things are the most powerful.

Let's pick a topic for an example where we can use these questions.

How I Solved a Very Big Problem

———

I had a serious problem when it came to marrying the woman I love!

When I met my wife, I soon knew that I wanted to marry her, but we faced a lot of challenges. First, she was just visiting here learning English for a year and her father didn't like the idea of her moving to Canada. He wanted her to live in Korea.

When she went back to Korea I paid a lot of extra money calling her. Even though she had her own cell phone I called the house line and talked with her father first so he could get to know me.

I also had to learn how to speak Korean better and deal

with some of the cultural differences between us.

I even had to smooth the way in my own family by convincing them what a good fit she would be with us.

Here's how I solved the problem using the 5 W's — I asked myself:

What is the problem? — Her dad doesn't want her to move to Canada.

Why doesn't he want that? — He will miss her and won't be around to make sure she's ok.

How can I ease his mind that I will take good care of her?

Where can we make some compromises that will make him more agreeable?

Who can I get on my side to talk him into it?

When is the best time to talk to him so he might be in a more agreeable mood?

I think you get the idea where I'm going here. You could use this for how to lose weight:

What do I weigh right now? **What** do I want to weigh?

Why am I putting on the pounds? — Not enough exercise and too much late-night Ramen!

How can I start changing my habits? — Change the ramen for a protein shake, and make a time to work out

Where can I go to work out? — Build my own butt-kickin' home gym in my garage!

Who can I get to support me in working out and eating right? — make a post on Facebook and challenge my friends to come work out with me.

Get creative and have fun with your questions. Your brain likes to create and play. Sometimes we're too serious when we're trying to solve problems.

Let's talk about some more great ways to leverage the power of questions.

Brainstorming and Masterminding

Take the time to pull out a paper and pen, a whiteboard, or a Word document, whatever works for you, and just brainstorm. Asking the W questions is a form of brainstorming, but so is just writing a problem on the board and writing down random thoughts and questions and showing your train of thought. Sometimes that helps you get past the analytical side of your brain to come up with creative and unconventional answers.

Another good practice, of almost any highly successful person you talk to, is tapping into the power of masterminding.

Many good books on business growth encourage people

to form a mastermind group, which is a group of people that get together and brainstorm about a certain topic or problem. It's leveraging the power of good questions by giving them to a group and getting more than one brain working on solutions.

It's exciting to experience what happens when the right group of people get together. As we gather, the energy and synergy in the room kind of rubs off on one another so we can achieve more. It also gives each other permission and encouragement to dream and hope again.

For instance, with this book, I had the idea for it a long time. I started out with one other person who had a better gift for writing than I had, and the two of us started to bring it to life. Then I pulled in more of my friends for a mastermind session and we got more ideas that helped it to become even better.

Assessment is about using your brain. It's about actually

kicking your brain into a higher gear by asking it the right questions. It's about being honest with yourself and finding out where you are, where you want to be and how you're going to get there.

It's about examining the things you're doing, and why, then deciding which things are your top priority and focusing on them while letting other non-essential activities go. We need to stop merely existing and going with the flow — just reacting to life — and take a personal inventory of our day so far.

I'd recommend you take just five or ten minutes, either in the morning, at lunch or coffee-break, in the evening at supper, or before bed, to assess whether you're on track with your use of time.

Use good questions to ask yourself "Am I open to, and looking for, new opportunities? Am I getting the things done today that I set out to do? Could I use some attitude adjustments? Am I investing my time wisely? If not, what can I do differently?"

Being brutally honest with oneself is vital to real growth. At the same time, be gracious and loving in your judgements. Don't wallow in guilt or regret about your mistakes. Forgive yourself, realize that you're still growing, and don't expect perfection!

> "Being entirely honest with oneself is a good exercise."
>
> — Sigmund Freud, Austrian neurologist and
> the founder of psychoanalysis
>
> "To save myself I must face myself, which may be the hardest of all things to face."
>
> — Craig D. Lounsbrough, Author, Speaker, Licensed Professional Counselor, Certified Professional Life Coach, Ordained Minister

We're not animals just reacting to exterior influences. We have the ability to think and affect the world around us. That's our God-given gift that differentiates us from any other species, right?

The whole purpose of 'Assessment' is taking quiet time to

reflect and prioritize. This is just common sense, but again, unfortunately, it's not common practice!

There are more and more distractions nowadays, with smartphones, social media, and the internet. Everyone, and everything, is vying for our attention, but we must give attention to our lives if we want a life worth living!

Make quiet reflection time a mandatory habit in your day.

The Power of Self-Assessment

The skill of self-assessment is showing impressive results in improving the quality of work in school children. Teachers have found that creating self-assessment tools for children to measure their assignments by themselves encourages a higher level of work.

Instead of just getting the teacher's judgement of something with a red x, checkmark, or grade, they can look at something that shows the expectations, and then readjust their work accordingly. They get to choose to raise their work to a higher standard, instead of just handing something in with a minimum of effort. They assess and challenge themselves.

Many of us go through life robotically, just receiving the judgements and standards of others. I think we should create our own self-assessment tools that will encourage us to take our own measure, and adjust and correct where necessary.

"If you keep doing what you've always done, you'll keep getting what you've always got."
— Jack Canfield, American author, motivational speaker, seminar leader, corporate trainer, and entrepreneur

Taking a few moments to invest your time in self-assessment can save you years of being stuck in the insanity trap of doing the same thing and dreaming of different results. Remember, time is valuable. It is a finite commodity. When opportunity knocks, it doesn't stand by the door waiting. Make sure you are taking regular assessments on how you are developing your use of time and opportunity.

Our next section is broken into two parts.

It's about your **Yield**, the most exciting and rewarding part of TODAY - the fruits of your labor that you and the world can enjoy after you've done the rest of the steps in using TODAY well.

Assignments for Assessing your Actions:

Assignment 1 Create a daily and pre-week assessment grid

Try using something like Darren Hardy's Sunday Planning System to map out your week before it begins. Then each morning use Stephen Covey's 4 Quadrants to map out your day keeping to the Urgent-Important and Not Urgent but Important sections.

Assignment 2 Plan some assessment times

Carve out a few small blocks of time in your day for assessing your day as you go. Set a timer on your phone or another device to think about your day so far. You know what times would work best according to your schedule. Don't *wait* for a time. *Make* a time. Ignore your phone or other distractions for a moment and just look back and think. Ask yourself how you think you're doing. Are you sticking to the most important things you need to be doing to move forward with your goals? Make some notes of thoughts or ideas that come to you.

Think of it as the breaks in a boxing match; rest in the corner for a minute and strategize on the moves you need to make to win.

After your breather, get back into the ring, and adjust your punches as necessary! Think about how you've been doing today, shake off the pain of blows you've received and get a new strategy,

I recommend that you also set regular assessment times throughout the year. Get out your calendar or yearly planner, and set a time once a week, once a month, quarterly, and once a year, to do bigger overall assessments of your time use.

"The only way to make a spoilt machine work again is to break it down, work on its inner system and fix it again. Screw out the bolts of your life, examine and work on yourself, fix your life again and get going."

— *Israelmore Ayivor, Founder of IPDLA which Trains, and Awards Young Leaders Globally*

Yield²

The two keys to exponential growth

Now we're going to look at the two forms of Yield that, when used together, have exponential power!

You will notice that the word Yield is squared, or to the power of 2.

Math might not be your strong suit, so here's a short explanation: An exponent refers to the number of times a number is multiplied by itself. For example:

2 to the 3rd power (written like this: 2^3) means:

$2 \times 2 \times 2 = 8$.

2^3 is not the same as 2×3 (= 6), it has a larger sum.

When you get into larger numbers the final sum can be staggering!

For instance:

10 to the power of 10, multiplying 10 by itself 10 times = 10,000,000,000

That's ten billion!

The word 'exponential' describes an extremely rapid increase. I think we'd all like to have an extremely rapid increase in the results of our efforts, so let's take a look!

1st Yield:
To Produce

How to create a 'success machine'

"The best way to assess yourself is to base the assessment on the product you produce daily."

— *Sunday Adelaja, founder and senior pastor of the Embassy of the
Blessed Kingdom of God for All Nations*

We've talked about forms of measurement. TODAY is measured in increments of time — hours and minutes. Those
hours and minutes can also be measured by the energy
we put into them. We each only have a finite amount of
physical, mental and emotional life energy for each day. If
you waste your energy by using it on the wrong things, you

waste your day.

Our life can be measured in time and accomplishments.

Our daily Yield — the actual things we produce, is the perfect self-assessment measuring tool. We need to have the mindset that each and every day we must produce something that can be measured — a unit of something that's tangible.

> "You don't actually do a project; you can only do action steps related to it. When enough of the right action steps have been taken, some situation will have been created that matches your initial picture of the outcome closely enough that you can call it 'done.'"
>
> — *David Allen, productivity consultant and creator of the time management method known as "**Getting Things Done**"*

It really helps to have a goal that can easily be measured. If you want a fit body, you need to do specific actions to achieve it. Most people find that having a plan to follow helps them.

If you eat a certain number of calories - that can be measured. If you do bicep curls with a certain amount of reps, sets, and weight, and keep track of it, then you know what you have to do next to push yourself. If you continue doing these measurable things, you will eventually have the results you want.

If you have an idea, then write it down - that's a measurable thing. Getting it from your brain to paper starts to bring it to life. Maybe from there, you can make a prototype, meet a person, or make a phone call and set a meeting date. Whatever it is, we have the gift, and the power, to will our ideas into existence.

Producing every single day comes down to the first T — Time. It's finite — we can't do it tomorrow. Pretend like tomorrow doesn't exist.

When you wake up in the morning, you should be filled with thankfulness and gratitude that you have another day. That day, before the sun goes down, make sure you produce at least one thing. Make sure you bring something into existence that is tangible.

There's an excellent story the actor Will Smith tells about this principle of bringing something into existence one measurable activity at a time.

Just One Brick

———

When Will was a kid, his dad decided that he wanted to replace the large front wall in his shop. It was about 16 ft. high by 30 ft. wide. He gave the daunting task to Will and his younger brother! They had to dig a 6-foot hole, start mixing cement, and laying brick.

They did it every day after school, and at one point in time Will thought there would be a giant hole in that wall forever! It took those boys a year and a half, but they did it!

When they were done and standing there looking at it with their father, their dad said, "Don'tcha all never tell me you can't do something!"

Will says, "I learned very young from my parents that you don't try to build a wall. You don't set out to build a wall. You don't say 'I'm going to build the biggest, baddest, greatest wall that's ever been built.'

You don't start there. You say 'I'm going to lay this brick as perfectly as a brick can be laid. There's not gonna be one brick on the face of this earth that's going to be laid better than this brick that's gonna be laid!' And you do that every single day, and soon you'll have a wall.

Psychologically, the advantage that gives me over a lot of people that I've been in competition with is, it's difficult to take the first step when you look at how big the task is. It's always just that One Brick."

This is a perfect picture of producing one thing well each

day, every day, even when it seems like the big picture will never be completed!

If two boys can build a large brick wall one day at a time after school, you can build your dream one 'brick' at a time too. Each little success will lead to the next, until you have something awesome.

A friend of mine told me a story that fits with Will Smith's Just One Brick story. He said he had a friend who went to Africa to do some not-for-profit work. They were getting discouraged that things weren't going as well or as quickly as they would have liked to see. They felt like giving up until a wise old African man told her a proverb. He said, "Brick by brick, slowly by slowly".

I had to dig myself out of the huge debt I created by my mistake slowly, paycheck by paycheck. I wished it could have happened faster, but I kept at it faithfully and now it's gone and I've gotten myself way ahead. I didn't give up.

A Different Kind of Little Engine That Could
— The Power of a Small Success

———

There's a children's story about a little train engine called 'The Little Engine That Could'. The Little Engine was having trouble getting up a hill. She eventually just kept chugging up the hill saying "I think I can, I think I can, I think I can!" until she reached the top.

There is another little engine that has an interesting purpose.

Large bulldozers used to need a small gasoline engine to help turn over their larger diesel engine until it could run on its own. Once those big machines get going, they have the power to do some pretty big jobs, but it takes something small to get them started!

Small successes help generate the power to get the bigger engine of our dreams running! Each little thing you do towards your goal creates a positive energy in you that gives you the fuel you need to work on the next one.

For me, in the beginning of my journey, just starting to use some of my talents and feeling like I was growing was a huge motivation, even when I couldn't see anything happening physically.

I failed at more things than I succeeded at, but I felt alive! Before that I felt like I had just been sleepwalking through life and now I was fully awake and running!

Not many things changed for me externally, and it didn't show in my bank account either, but I knew that something had changed within me. I was changing and thinking differently — just feeling like I was growing and changing was a win that helped fuel me to press on.

"Small wins lead to big victories."

— Jae Park

"Success is rarely the result of one swell swoop, but more often the culmination of many, many small victories."

— Joseph M. Marshall III, historian, writer, teacher, craftsman, administrator, actor, and public speaker

> "Look for small victories and build on that. Each small victory, even if it is just getting up five minutes earlier, gives you confidence. You realize that these little victories make you feel great, and you keep going. You realize that being paralyzed by fear of failure is worse than failure."
>
> *— Arnold Schwarzenegger, Austrian-American actor, filmmaker, businessman, investor, author, philanthropist, activist, politician, and former professional bodybuilder and powerlifter*

Good coaches and teachers know the power of helping their students start off with small wins. They give them easy tasks that they know they can do, so their student gets excited with the feeling of accomplishment, and it gives them the confidence to take the next step!

So, what is your first step?

Just get the ball rolling, and do that one first thing, then the next, and so on!

Remember, if it's worth doing, it's worth doing **now**, so make your dreams and ideas come to life one unit of measurable effort at a time.

That's what the Yield mindset is — to **prime** yourself to produce something. Making sure that you actually produce something tangible before you finish the day is important. Make sure you're priming your brain to really produce!

> "Being busy does not always mean real work. The object of all work is production or accomplishment and to either of these ends there must be forethought, system, planning, intelligence, and honest purpose, as well as perspiration. Seeming to do is not doing."
>
> — *Thomas A. Edison, American inventor and businessman*

An 'intangible' Brick I Lay Every Day

I know I said to do tangible and measurable things that can have measurable results, but some things aren't as easy to measure, and seem intangible, yet are just as important to do.

For instance, building closeness with the people around you is something that we all need to work on. Sometimes we can go through the day and not tell our family that you we love them. We can be in proximity to them but not verbalize it.

You should take every opportunity to let the important people in your life know that you love them. That's something relation-wise that I always try to do — to take the time to say "Hey, I love you. I care about you. You're special to me." It yields the results of a closer connection with those you care about.

The next and last section, the second part of Yield, is the thing that multiplies all this action and use of time and opportunity exponentially.

It's the golden key, based on the golden rule — "Do unto others as you would have them do unto you!"

Assignments for Producing every day

Assignment 1 Write down your wins, no matter how small

At the end of your day, or at your assessment times, write down everything you feel was a tangible, or measurable result.

Don't focus on what you haven't done yet, don't think of 'the wall', just note each 'brick' you've laid! Give yourself a pat on the back for what you've done, even the little things!

If you can, post it where you can see it, so it will encourage you. Seeing progress gives you hope and enthusiasm to keep going.

2nd Yield:
To Serve and Submit

**Success at the service of others,
not at the expense of others**

Serve

"The law of sowing and reaping is that you will reap what you sow, and you will reap more than you sow."

Sowing seed is an exciting and amazing thing. All you have to do is stick one seed in the ground and you eventually harvest many more seeds than you planted. One grain of wheat or corn produces a stalk with many new grains on it so you always reap more than you sow. It's a natural principle of growth that works in every area of life.

The other half of the 'growth law' is that you will reap what you sow. For instance, if you sow corn seed, you won't harvest wheat — what you plant is what you get. Some people expect good things to come their way without ever doing good things for someone else! It doesn't work that way.

Other people seem to expect a harvest without ever doing the work of planting anything — instead, they're waiting to win a lottery!

This final section of our look at The Power of TODAY is really where you should begin everything in your life. The truth in this section is the foundation for success in all the others, and adds the exponential power of multiplication to everything in your life.

It's the power of doing everything we do for the benefit of others rather than at the expense of others, and sowing more into your own life, by sowing seeds of kindness into the lives of others.

> "Give, and it will be given to you.
> A good measure, pressed down, shaken together and
> running over, will be poured into your lap. For with the
> measure you use, it will be measured to you."
>
> — *Jesus, Luke 6:38 (NIV)*

I'm not religious, but I'm spiritual. I'm a God-follower. I submit myself to God. He wants us all to serve each other. Jesus was God's perfect example of what it looks like to serve and lay down your own life for others.

It's not always easy to do that. It doesn't always seem like the most profitable thing to do at the time! Serving others always costs us something, like time, energy, or our own desires.

Whether we want to admit it or not, no matter what our belief system is, we all struggle with selfishness at times. A lot of what we do can stem from the selfish motives of meeting our own needs. The problem is that if we're doing things only for ourselves, it won't take us very far. We need to make value for other people and serve others if we want to see the best and most rewarding growth in our lives.

I might do things for myself, but my strength and willpower to do something for my children or my wife is much stronger!

You have to bring value to other people. You have to be successful at the service of others, not at the expense of others. When you are focused on other people's needs, wants, and desires, things come really easy to you. That's when you start attracting success. That's when you start attracting money.

When your motive is selfish, you can strive to get rich and achieve it, yet lose something even more valuable and important!

This concept of really serving others and delivering value to them first can be very foreign sometimes. We are taught to look after ourselves first, but when you put others ahead of yourself, you will find that things will go well for you. It's a success principal that most of the 'truly successful' people know and live by.

"The first question which the priest and the Levite asked was: 'truly I stop to help this man, what will happen to me?' But the good Samaritan reversed the question: 'If I do not stop to help this man, what will happen to him?'"

— Martin Luther King Jr., American Baptist minister and activist who became the most visible spokesperson and leader in the civil rights movement

"You need an attitude of service. You're not just serving yourself. You help others to grow up and you grow with them."

— David Green, American businessman, philanthropist, and the founder of Hobby Lobby

"The more generous we are, the more joyous we become. The more cooperative we are, the more valuable we become. The more enthusiastic we are, the more productive we become. The more serving we are, the more prosperous we become."

— William Arthur Ward, one of America's most quoted writers of inspirational maxims

It takes faith to give to others, especially when you, yourself, are in need. I'm reminded of the story in the Bible, about a woman and her son that were caught in a severe famine because of a draught in the land. All they had left was enough food for one more meal — then, they would probably die of starvation.

She was told that if she gave some of her last meal to the prophet Elijah, then fed herself and her son, that her supply would never run out! She chose to believe it, and at a time when no one else had enough, her oil and flour never ran dry!

Putting others first makes way for miracles!

Priming Takes Faith

There's an old story about a man riding a long way in the desert with no water who stumbles across a well. He finds a jar of water beside the well and wants to drink it but there's a note on the jar that says the water is for priming the pump. It says the pump works but you need to use the water to get it going.

The man was so thirsty and didn't really want to take the chance of wasting that small jar of water, but he decided to prime the pump with it and was able to get all the water he needed to drink, cool and wash himself, and water his horse.

The note on the jar also reminded him to fill the jar again and leave it for the next person to prime the pump with.

Giving first and serving others is how you prime and prepare the way for a free flow of real abundance and prosperity in your life.

We've been using the word prime a lot in this book. We need to prime our minds to be open to opportunities, prime ourselves to create a 'brick' every day, and prime our hearts to be givers so we can receive an abundance!

If we don't prime the pump, it will run the motor without drawing any water.

Sometimes we're working hard and not getting anywhere. We need to stop and assess what our motives are, what we're doing, and whether we are giving value to others.

Maybe we haven't properly primed our mind and heart so there can be a free flow of the things we really want. We need to have faith that if we prime the pump by serving others first, there will be more than enough for us.

Submit

"Submission is not about authority and it is not obedience; it is all about relationships of love and respect."
— *William Paul Young, author of **The Shack***

Definition of submit:
Accept or yield to a superior force or to the authority or will of another person

If you read the definition of the word submit above, the part I'm talking about is yielding to a superior force. The superior force that I encourage you to yield to is Love. I think most of us would agree that love is the most powerful force in a person's life. Ultimately, love conquers all.

The Bible says that God *is* love. Whether you believe in God, and choose to surrender to his will, which is for us all to love one another, or you just believe in the power of love and its effects on mankind, I think you'll agree that learning to live a life based on love is the best life to have!

Love isn't a feeling, although good emotions are a by-product of it. Love is expressed in action, in all the kind things we do. It is also expressed in self-control, and *not* doing things that our emotional reactions tell us to do!

For instance, exercising patience and forgiveness is an act of love. If you are a parent, you'll understand that love is often expressed through sacrifice — through laying down your needs and desires for others. Love is serving others rather than just serving your own needs.

The golden rule — 'Do unto others as you would have them do unto you' — is the mandate of love.

If you submit your life to the superior force of love, you will reap love's rewards, which are an abundance of every truly good thing.

Love's rewards can't be taken away from you. You can lose money and things, but the worth of peace, a clear conscience, and the appreciation and affection of others, can't be measured, or taken away!

When you submit to the power of serving others in love, your Yield will be greatly increased!

I truly hope that reading this book on The Power of TO-DAY^2, has been, and will continue to be, a valuable investment of your time.

I've included a page at the end with a poster of the acronym TODAY.

You can print it out, and post it somewhere, to remind you to do the things it stands for every day, so you can see the successful fulfillment of your dreams and goals.

Thank you for taking a chance on me by reading this book.

I hope it proves to be the opportunity you needed to get yourself in gear to squeeze out every precious moment of TODAY and get all you can out of the time you have left!

I look forward to hearing about the Yield you will one day enjoy and share with the world.

It has been a rewarding use of my time in writing it for you.

Yours truly,

Jae Park

TODA(Y)² Chart

If it's worth doing, it's worth doing NOW, because you might not have tomorrow!

Time —

is a gift — your most precious commodity

Opportunity —

is everywhere, every day, if you're primed for it

Development —

your personal growth is the quickest and surest way to success

Assessment —

should be done every day to keep you on track for your goals

Yield^2 —

Yield 1: to Produce —

at least one measurable unit every single day!

Yield 2: to Serve and Submit —

be successful at the service of others not at the expense of others